The Wisdom of Ginsu®

Carve Yourself a Piece of the American Dream

The Wisdom of Ginsu®

Carve Yourself a Piece of the American Dream

By

Barry Becher and Edward Valenti
The Ginsu Guys™

CAREER
PRESS
Franklin Lakes, NJ

THE WISDOM OF GINSU
EDITED AND TYPESET BY KRISTEN PARKES
Cover design by DesignConcept
Printed in the U.S.A. by Book-mart Press
Ginsu is a registered trademark of the Douglas Quikut
division of the Scott Fetzer Company
Commercial photos courtesy of Longstreet Photo Reports

To order this title, please call toll-free 1-800-CAREER-1 (NJ and Canada: 201-848-0310) to order using VISA or MasterCard, or for further information on books from Career Press.

CAREER
PRESS

The Career Press, Inc., 3 Tice Road, PO Box 687,
Franklin Lakes, NJ 07417
www.careerpress.com

Library of Congress Cataloging-in-Publication Data
Available upon request.

Acknowledgments

Over the last 30 years, one of the most important lessons we have learned is that there are always two ways to look at things…and the truth is most often found somewhere in the middle.

This certainly is the case when it comes to the common characteristics of successful entrepreneurs: On one hand, we're often described as competitive, self-motivated, open to risk, independent, self-confident, creative, multi-taskers who love a challenge and who, in pursuit of predetermined dreams and goals, work long hours, possess a strong sense of self-worth, have lots of energy, enjoy a challenge, and appreciate the value of a dollar. On the other, far less charitable hand, we entrepreneurs are called ruthless, self-centered, relentlessly driven risk-takers who are egotistical, rule-breaking, dreamers and workaholics, headed off in a million different directions at once, intentionally seeking out obstacles and creating new ones, all in order to achieve obscene levels of financial wealth.

No matter where our entrepreneurial characteristics fall between those two extremes, on a personal level we are very fortunate to share our lives with some very special individuals who know that, first and foremost, we are good people with good hearts who just happen to also be very good at business.

These people always see the best in us and love us for the type of people we are (not the type of businesspersons we are labeled as).

They have seen us at our best and at our worst as entrepreneurs and human beings, and have chosen firmly to support us, love us, follow us, and believe in us over many, many years; our lives and careers would be meaningless without them. We, of course, are talking about our accountants…um, we mean our lovely wives, Leslie Becher and Brenda Valenti.

Heartfelt thanks and sincere appreciation, Leslie and Brenda, for all that you have done to love us and support us, for keeping the home fires burning, and for choosing to see the best in us, each and every day. Know that we love you always and appreciate the many ways you make our lives worth living. Thank you especially for your support during the writing of this book.

We'd also like to thank our daughters, Erica and Erin (Valenti), Lisa and Kim (Becher); stepdaughters (Jodi and Stacy); grandkids; as well as all of our sons-in-law (Joe, Ken, Craig, Mike, and Kurt), for all the joy they've brought into our lives, for the love they have for us and our grandchildren, and for giving us a reason to get up and go to work every day and an even better reason to stay home and play hooky once in a while! You have all helped us in different ways, along the way, and we love you all dearly.

Now to our thanks specifically in the writing of this book: First on the list is James J. Cooney Jr.

Jimmy, in many ways, is responsible for this book. He not only helped organize our thoughts but helped us to clarify, list, and name our "Ginsuisms" (personal and professional lessons and pearls of wisdom) and put them into words. He also was the keeper of the Ginsu archives (photos, articles, etc.) before we even knew that we were going to need archives for this and other projects. Jim was the first to dub us "The Ginsu Guys™" (and to tell us to make sure we trademarked the name). He invested many hours of advice, inspiration, creative direction, editing, and faith in this project…and in us. Perhaps an even larger part of Jim's contribution has been his dedication to us as this story was unfolding over the last 25 years. In short, Jim was, and is, the glue that holds us together. Whenever Barry and I had a dispute, over the years or during the writing of this book, he would chuckle, shake his head, and mutter, "Looks like Godzilla and Rodan are going at it again!" At some of our toughest moments he would find a way to make us laugh at our problems and ourselves. The man has the patience of JOB! Thanks, Jim.

Second is Shelley Roth, our agent. Or, as we like to call her, the "Terminator" agent, because no matter what happens, she never quits and always comes "back." Thanks, Shelley, for sticking with us, believing in this story, and making this book deal happen. Thanks also for your patience with two entrepreneurs with hundreds of questions, even more suggestions, and all of the "interesting" qualities and characteristics mentioned at the beginning of these acknowledgments. As we often say, "Just think, instead of only working with us, you could have to live with us!" Feel better? Thought so.

Third is Cemal Ekin, our dear friend for many years. From the time we first met him, he's always been there for us on a number of different levels. His technical wizardry is unequaled. He is the guru of gurus. His input definitely helped, and his output in formatting this document was invaluable. And special thanks to Ed's daughter Erica for coming up with the subtitle "Carve Yourself a Piece of the American Dream."

And finally, we would like to thank our customers. First, all the people who bought our Ginsu knives and our other TV direct marketing products. Without you, we'd be broke, we certainly wouldn't have the chance to write this book, and marketing history would be a lot less fun and not nearly as interesting!

And second, all the people who bought this book and are reading it now. We hope you enjoy the business, personal, and life lessons we have picked up along the way and that you somehow find a way to use them to write the next chapter in your own personal and professional success story! Nothing would make us happier at this stage of our lives than passing along the torch of entrepreneurial success!

Contents

Introduction

Right about now you're probably saying to yourself, "Okay, so they sold a gazillion Ginsu knives, but how does that qualify them to tell me how to run a more successful business or lead a better life?" Well first of all, they aren't going to "tell" you how to do anything. They are only going to tell you how they did a lot of successful and not so successful things—what they learned from it and what you can learn from it. What you do with that information is really up to you. Ed and Barry asked me to write this Introduction because I've been working for, and with, them for more than 25 years, right out of college. Although they've worked with literally thousands of people over the years, nobody on the planet has worked with them longer, learned more, or seen more. So, I guess I'm what you'd call a living, breathing, customer testimonial. As their primary pupil over the last quarter century, I was the logical choice to help Ed and Barry encapsulate some of the most valuable pieces of information and lessons that I learned from them into the 24 Ginsuisms discussed in this book. So, before you decide what qualifies the "Ginsu Guys" to offer this type of information, please read the rest of this Introduction. Once you do, I think you'll understand completely. I know I wouldn't trade the personal and professional education they've given me over the last 25 years for a free ride to Harvard Business School. In case you're thinking that they probably paid me to say that, let me tell you, they didn't. However, learning how they got me to say that, without paying me a penny, is worth more than the price of this entire book! If I were to attend Harvard Business School, I'm sure that one of the first things they would teach me is to find a mentor, someone who can guide you along the way, teach you the ins and outs of being successful, and help lead you through the obstacle course of business and life. The only problem is, how do you find the right mentor, someone who can teach you everything you need to know to be successful in your personal and professional lives? Well, if you read this book, you won't have to look any further because you'll have found two of the greatest mentors around...so, start reading!

The Ginsu Years

In 1975, a young, ambitious broadcasting executive (Ed Valenti) for a local NBC affiliate television station in Providence, Rhode Island, and an enterprising, young AAMCO Transmission shop entrepreneur (Barry Becher) put their heads together, teamed up, and forever changed the way products are marketed on television. Theirs was a partnership that would achieve incredible monetary success, usher in a new era of marketing and communications, and revolutionize the direct response industry and the way products are sold on television forever! Their zany yet clever commercials—advertising such products as the Miracle Painter, Armourcote cookware, and, most famously, the Ginsu knife—quickly captured both the imagination and pocketbook of the American public. Their commercials featured such antics as karate-chopping tomatoes and dropping a raw egg on a diamond ring, and gave birth to such familiar phrases as "But wait, there's more!" and "Now how much would you pay?"—phrases now permanently embedded in the American vernacular.

Barry, a middle-class kid from Brooklyn, New York, and Ed, a poor, ambitious kid from Fall River, Massachusetts, defied the experts, challenged the naysayers, and made marketing history while staying true to themselves, and to each other.

And they became millionaires in the process.

What a Country!

Ed and Barry's direct marketing company was opened in 1975, and, as a result of the enormous reaction to their ads, they proceeded to develop many multimillion selling and "Miraculous" products including the Miracle Slicer, the Miracle Duster, Claudette Louberge Hosiery, Royal DuraSteel, Vacufresh, the Chainge adjustable necklace, Lustreware flatware, Armourcote cookware, and, of course, the legendary Ginsu knives.

Thanks to the tremendous success of these products, their company went from being a part-time operation run out of Barry's garage to being one of the largest buyers of spot television in the country, with more than 150 employees and 20 to 30 products on the air in just about every market in the country at any given time. Ed and Barry spent millions of their own money every quarter on ads all over America. In fact, their expenditure ranked them just ahead of Coca-Cola and right behind AT&T on the list of America's top ad spenders in national spot TV markets! Total sales for the enterprising duo's products, over a 10-year period, was more than $500 million!

Why was Ed and Barry's method of direct response advertising so successful? Their outrageous, extraordinary, and oftentimes comical commercials were a major contributor to that success, although that was far from being the only reason. The times chosen to run the ads, the research that went into the creation of the ads, the stations and programs that were chosen, the use of toll-free 800 numbers, the acceptance of credit card orders, and the daily and weekly result analysis and invoice reconciliation methods were all revolutionary direct marketing techniques pioneered and established by Ed and Barry.

What's more, their unique style of product presentation and demonstration and insider's knowledge of media-buying techniques and strategies not only made them very successful, it made them profitable beyond their wildest dreams…and known throughout the world.

A Cut Above

Most of the products developed by Ed and Barry were incredibly successful, but only one has transcended its own success and evolved into a genuine cultural icon: the most memorable product ever promoted on TV, Ginsu knives! It is largely due to comedians that Ginsu, to this day (more than 20 years after the commercials last aired), is one of the most mentioned and well-known products in history. Gallagher made a career out of mimicking the commercial's antics; Jerry Seinfeld did a routine on Ginsu on *The Tonight Show with Jay Leno* the night of his show's last episode; Johnny Carson used it as a standing part of his nightly routine for years; Joe Piscopo, John Belushi, Phil Hartman, and Dan Aykroyd all incorporated Ginsu into skits on *Saturday Night Live*; even Tony Soprano has mentioned Ginsu when seated at the "family" dinner table on the HBO series *The Sopranos*; and the comic strip "The Wizard of Id" and *The New Yorker* magazine cartoons routinely featured Ginsu references. Mentions in movies such as *Teenage Mutant Ninja Turtles*, *Sleepless in Seattle*, and *Scrooged* with Bill Murray, as well as television sitcoms, are simply too numerous to mention. In addition, Ed, Barry, Ginsu, and their other TV products have recently been featured in numerous documentaries on national television networks ranging from ABC (Chronicle) and The History Channel to The Discovery Channel and The Arts and Entertainment (A&E) Network, and VH1's *Pop-Up Video* and *I love the 70's*.

The Legend Lives On

In fact, it is clear that Ed and Barry's creation, the Ginsu knife, has become a worldwide household name. Why? Maybe it was the catchy yet totally fabricated, Japanese-sounding name or the impossible to ignore ads or the colorful, rapid-fire copy. Or perhaps it was the incredible versatility, sharpness, and durability of the knife itself! Whatever the reason, one thing is certain: people remember Ginsu, the kitchen cutting tool that can "cut through a nail, a tin can, and a radiator hose and still slice a tomato paper thin." Alas, even the world's greatest legends are not completely immune from the harsh light of reality, which is why it probably won't surprise you to learn that Ginsu, the most famous "Japanese" product ever sold, was really manufactured in Freemont, Ohio, by the Quikut Division of Scott & Fetzer. Today Ginsu is owned by Wall Street wizard Warren Buffett, one of the wealthiest and most successful men in America.

The "Ginsu Guys" Today...and the Lessons They Leave Behind

Hitting it big even once in America's competitive business environment is an extraordinary feat; doing it twice is almost unheard of; and three times (in three completely different industries) is beyond comprehension. Yet, today Ed and Barry are the cofounders and owners of a successful media-buying and marketing firm, PriMedia Inc., which has just marked its 15th successful year in business. Prior to that, Barry and Ed "hit it big" as a multiple-location franchise owner and top broadcast sales representative/account executive, respectively, and then as co-owners of one of America's most successful direct response marketing firms.

In an effort to pass the torch of personal and professional wisdom they have gleaned from nearly 30 years of business success on to future entrepreneurs and business professionals, Ed and Barry have written *The Wisdom of Ginsu: Carve Yourself a Piece of the American Dream*. It is a valuable collection of life lessons, timeless tips, and pearls of wisdom, combined with interesting anecdotes and real-life business encounters they experienced (and learned from) along the way!

Barry and Ed were just a couple of green kids when they started. There were no precedents to guide them when they wrote those televised sales pitches, set up answering services and warehouses nationwide, created a company that employed hundreds and made millions, and pioneered marketing techniques that are still in widespread use today. They had to invent them. Along the way they had a lot of great successes and a few embarrassing failures, but with each step forward or back, they learned something. These lessons have been dubbed Ginsuisms—commonsense, back-to-basic approaches to life and business, things that seem to be disappearing in today's world. Compiled in this book, Ginsuisms create an instruction manual for life and the lost art of dealing with people.

Ed and Barry believe that the more technologically advanced we get, the more important it becomes not to lose touch with the basics of interpersonal relationships and business practices. As an example, it's far too easy today to send an e-mail or fax, or leave a voice-mail message instead of speaking to someone directly. They call these technological advances WMC (Weapons of Mass Communications) simply because they can silently kill your business without your knowledge. Their techniques are even more important today than they were years ago. The wisdom that they will share with you in this book has been, and continues to be, the cornerstone of their success.

In this fun and very readable book, Barry and Ed offer their top 24 hard-earned Ginsuisms. They provide explanations of each one, following each with entertaining behind-the-scenes stories of their incredible rise to success as well as the challenges and obstacles they faced along the way.

Irreverent, instructive, often with attitude, sometimes tongue-in-cheek, *The Wisdom of Ginsu* offers the reader the successful nuggets of wisdom that the authors used for years to stay one step ahead of the crowd and earn millions of dollars. Their book will teach readers to grab the bull by the horns and to think about situations in a different light by providing the reader with the authors' own real-life examples of business deals, relationships, challenges, and other "problems" they faced throughout their remarkable business career, as well as their often ingenious solutions.

In addition to being a blueprint for successful business strategies, *The Wisdom of Ginsu* is an entertaining, informative, and practical guide for everyday life. It's Dale Carnegie's *How to Win Friends and Influence People* for the 21st century.

Caution! Ed and Barry pull no punches. In fact, throughout the book, in order to give you a realistic glimpse at the interactive nature of their thinking, partnership, and thought process, Ed and Barry alternately offer you Ginsuisms, observations, anecdotes, and recollections, uncensored, that fully illustrate and define each chapter.

But wait, there's more! Ed and Barry discuss everything from getting a better price on anything you buy to getting better service; how to get bumped from coach to first class on an airline; why you should expect more from yourself and those around you, and how to get it; how to decide who to hire and who to fire; how to get phone calls returned; how to help yourself by helping others; where to find unexpected cash flow; who to trust and who to trump; and much, much more!

How much would you pay for all the secrets of business and professional success in the 2000s?

Don't answer! Because the sooner you start reading *The Wisdom of Ginsu*, the sooner you can start using the Ginsuisms contained within to build a better, and more successful, personal and professional life! But this is a limited time offer, so ACT NOW!

JIM COONEY, NOVEMBER 2004

P.S. One of the earliest and most important lessons (Ginsuisms) Ed and Barry learned became the basis of a successful business partnership and personal friendship of more than 30 years that generated hundreds of millions of dollars in sales and survived heart attacks, hospital stays, marriages, divorces, lost friendships, trust, betrayal, windfalls, bankruptcies, and retirement! You'll read all about it in Chapter 1....

Screen-Test Everyone...

Barry

Screen-test everyone...for the role they will play in your business and personal life. After all, most times first impressions truly are "as good as it gets." What you see in most people the first time you meet them is the best you will ever see. Good or bad! Why? Because that's how human nature works. It's natural, instinctive, and just the way it is. There's nothing you can do to change it, so your best bet is to accept it and learn from it.

Take the Hollywood screen test for example. The casting director or producer decides who gets the part by watching and listening to the actor act out the role. They don't make these decisions on the basis of whether or not someone will get better after he or she gets the part but instead on who performs the best during the screen test. No second chances here.

Same thing applies in real life as well. At first, mostly everyone works hard to make that first impression, but over time as human nature kicks in, many let down their guards and get comfortable and complacent about their jobs and relationships. Sort of like some first dates: great at first, downhill from there.

Ed

In business it's not that easy to find good people, and many companies hire employees, ignoring their negative first impressions, with the hope that the new hire will improve. Once in a while you may find someone who does actually improve, but most don't. In fact, most get worse. That's why we always relied on first impressions when hiring, picking a partner, or deciding with whom to work. If people aren't going to do all they can to impress you when there is incentive and pressure to do so, what can you expect when they get the job? At PriMedia, we once interviewed a person for a media position who showed up 45 minutes late. Throughout his entire interview, he never apologized.

When I finally asked, "What happened? Why didn't you call me?"

He said, "The traffic was terrible, and I didn't call because the battery in my cell phone went dead."

I guess all the pay phones in town were out of order too. If this person was giving me his best, what was his worst? As far as I was concerned, the interview was over right then and there. If he didn't have respect for me, how was he going to treat my customers?

Learn to trust your instincts, and don't overrule them. Most important of all, don't make excuses for people; they make enough for themselves. As a businessperson, you need to know that excuse-makers (including you) make excuses, not money. Don't believe me? Ask George Steinbrenner or Donald Trump. Does this mean that a proven performer can't offer you a legitimate excuse occasionally if something goes wrong? No. It simply means that if a person who is asking you for a job and who should be trying to make a good first impression, makes excuses instead, he is only going to do more of it once he starts working for you or with you. And if that person doesn't even attempt to make an excuse because he thinks his behavior is acceptable, recognize it and act accordingly. Your instincts are there for a reason, and first impressions are almost always right.

Instinct is actually how I found my business partner of the last 30 years. Barry was a guy that made a good impression from the start and kept it going. Here's what happened:

I was an account executive at the NBC TV station in Providence, and Barry was the owner of two AAMCO Transmission franchises in Rhode Island. Barry had left Brooklyn, New York, some years earlier with a boyhood friend to seek their fortune in the transmission business. (Although Barry and his partner did very well in this business, his fortune was not to be found under someone's car.)

Back at the TV station, the manager was shifting some accounts around and asked me if I wanted to handle the AAMCO account. He warned me that the owner was a real tough customer. Nevertheless, I still said yes.

The first time I drove up to his office and parked my orange Datsun 240Z (a very hot car at the time) next to his orange Datsun 240Z, I thought, "What a coincidence! This guy has class, too!"

I straightened my tie, and was ready to meet this potential nemesis. When I walked in, I was surprised to see a guy a few years older than myself, nice looking, wearing a mechanic's uniform with the name "Barry" on it. I quickly noticed that his nails were manicured.

"This guy isn't pulling out transmissions," I thought to myself. "He must be the owner."

I introduced myself and started to talk about the benefits of TV advertising over radio and newspaper. Barry cut me short and said in a firm but friendly manner, "Let's not waste time; put your best deal on the table, and if it's good enough, I'll buy it."

Although he had a reputation as a difficult person to do business with, he had a logical mind, and I knew I could appeal to it. After a short time, he was sold. Barry agreed to a summer schedule of newscasts and late-night spots, but I had to lower the rate substantially. My presentation was clear and logical. The resistance I expected never surfaced. In fact, I don't know why, but for some reason I was already starting to like him. His warm and friendly manner instantly made you feel like you were his friend and had known him for years. He simply wanted the best deal he could get and was willing to walk away when he felt he wasn't getting it.

Barry

Ed really seemed to know the TV business. He struck me as the most knowledgeable of all the people who had ever sold me advertising time. He knew the system inside and out, and where the loopholes were. It also seemed that he could change around my TV schedule almost at will. I would buy an inexpensive late-night TV spot, and somehow it would run in a very expensive Sunday NFL football game. If I bought a spot in the news, he would upgrade the spot to run in prime time without charging me any more money. His efforts were fantastic for my business.

In most cases unsold airtime is filled by showing a public service announcement, but Ed made sure that his clients' ads found their way into these unsold areas at a drastically reduced cost.

He would often say of his television job, "You do your best selling on the inside" of the television station.

The way he got his clients' spots shifted into prime-time slots was certainly proof of that.

I gained a great deal of respect for Ed's thinking and dedication as I continued to screen-test him. I really enjoyed his company and looked forward to his visits.

Ed

It was becoming quite clear that Barry had strengths in areas where I had weaknesses, and vice versa. One day at the shop he remarked that he had just finished his tax return and was getting a huge refund. I said, "I can't understand why I always have to pay."

He asked, "How much did you make last year and the year before?"

Normally I would never discuss my salary with anyone, let alone a client. I don't know why, but I blurted it out: "$40,000 last year, $25,000 the year before."

"Did you use income averaging?" Barry asked.

"No" I replied. "What the hell is income averaging?"

Barry asked me for copies of my tax returns for the last five years, and said, "If I get you some money back from the government, you owe me a dinner, agreed?" I agreed.

On the way back to the station, I started to question whether or not it was a good idea to tell Barry about my salary and, more importantly, whether or not I should have agreed to give him five years of tax returns. I told my wife, Brenda, that evening over dinner what happened and said, "I feel comfortable with Barry. I don't think he would reveal the information. He really seems to have a financial mind."

Brenda supported my feelings and told me to follow my instincts.

The next day Barry and I went over my tax returns in his office. After a few minutes of page turning and quick calculations he said, "You overpaid your taxes. I can get you around $1,000 back."

I was shocked and wasn't sure I believed him. After all, I thought I had a good accountant, and he had never said anything about income averaging.

Barry explained, "When you continuously make more money every year, you can average the five years together and pay taxes on the average."

He helped me fill out the proper forms to amend the return and we mailed them. Sure enough, a few weeks later I received a check from Uncle Sam for more than $1,000.

"Wow, this guy is pretty sharp," I thought.

It seemed that Barry was passing one screen test after another.

Barry

During our conversation I found out that Ed really loved sales. After all, he was young (only 26) and very confident. As one of the top billing salespeople in the market, he seemed to be the "golden boy" of television. He had only been working at Channel 10 for about six months, but he seemed to know the television business better than anyone I had ever met.

He had worked for five years as a radio account executive at the then Capital Cities, now ABC/Disney radio station, WPRO. It was the number-one station in town, and this apparently had made him sales-tough. With 17 radio stations in town to compete against, he had to be sharp and aggressive. No one could say anything he hadn't heard before; there didn't seem to be any objections he couldn't handle. I guess that's why the transition to TV had been so easy for him. He felt that television created an illusion for advertisers of being more important, bigger, and reputable. Everyone wanted to be associated with advertising in top television programs, they just didn't think it was within their financial reach. It was his job to show them the light, and, with his grasp of the industry and his work behind the scenes, he succeeded marvelously.

As the top billing sales executive of WPRO radio, he had negotiated the job at Channel 10 (NBC) from a position of strength and garnished the second biggest account list at the station. Though he had big accounts such as Coca-Cola, Mobil Oil, and several of the top agencies in town, he also had some smaller local accounts. Ed's goal was to convince me to lock into a long-term schedule and he sure was doing a great job of it.

Ed

At 26, I thought I was doing well: I had just bought my first house, two new cars, and had several thousand in the bank. But Barry had a plane, a business, and an old car on Nantucket Island in Massachusetts. That was out of my reach. Barry explained that when he first moved to Rhode Island to get one of the first AAMCO Transmission shops, he flew home to Brooklyn by commercial airline on weekends for dates and later bought his own plane to make the trip easier.

In my eyes, Barry had been the perfect bachelor: young, good-looking, with a few bucks, plus he had spent the first 23 years of his life living in the big city, New York. But what truly personified Barry's bachelorhood for me was when I learned that he never washed underwear (he wore them once and then threw them away). At the beginning of each month Barry would pick up his standing order of 30, 30, and 30: 30 pairs of underwear, 30 T-shirts, and 30 pairs of socks.

Whenever we ate together, Barry would always encourage me to leave more than the standard 15-percent tip. He would say, "These people really bust their buns and deserve all they get."

There was no set pattern emerging for me about him, hard in some ways, soft in others, and giving selectively. I was getting to like him more and more.

Barry

Later on I would find that wherever we traveled, be it Puerto Rico, Korea, or even Hong Kong, Ed's international good looks would have everyone thinking he was a native. Ed (being part Italian and part Portuguese) had a face that seemed to appeal to everyone.

In Mexico, when we ordered at restaurants, he was asked for his order in Spanish. When we took a cab, the same thing happened. At customs when departing Mexico, he was the only person who had to produce additional identification to get out of the country. We all got a good laugh out of that.

We had passed each other's screen test, but little did we realize at the time that fate would intervene and we would form a rare and unique partnership that would make history and generate $10 million in sales in its first year.

Ed

My screen test with Barry was right-on from the first minute I met him, and it's still right-on 30 years later. People often ask us how we've managed to stay partners and best friends all these years. Let's face it, very few marriages last that long. If you want a great relationship like Barry and I have, you have to get along, trust each other, respect each other, always put your friendship first...

...And "screen-test everyone."

If They Say It Can't Be Done. You'll Just Have to Do It Yourself!

Barry

Remember the old saying "if you want something done, do it yourself"? *It's true.* It is tough to motivate people, and most simply don't get it! Waiting for something to happen or someone to do something is wasteful and can be very expensive. Getting someone to even understand what you want done can sometimes be a problem. Many times Ed and I thought we spoke a different language. We would say it in English, and it seemed to get done in another language. Here's a good rule to remember when thinking about who should control your destiny: you! No one will ever have more passion for your project, job, career or future than *you*, or as much to win or lose. A stand-up comic tells a joke about people that is strikingly close to reality. It goes like this: "Half the world is critically stupid; now subtract 6 percent unemployment, and that means that 44 percent of the critically stupid people are working."

Given those numbers, there are quite a few of these folks you're going to come into contact with each day. Would you like to put your future in the hands of this group? I don't think so! Yet, many people do just that.

I'm sure every reader can tell a story (if you are honest with yourself) about someone you have come into contact with who fits this profile. We have all walked away from these encounters saying, "I cannot believe that person has a job. How stupid can one person be? I can't believe I took that advice!" And, "I should have done it myself!" Einstein once said that he found two infinites in life: human stupidity and the universe, but he wasn't so sure about the universe. The lesson here? Be prepared that, at times, you may need to do it yourself, and don't be upset when it happens. In the following story, I often think about what our life would have been like if we accepted the conclusions of what other people were saying about our future at the time. Both of us were convinced we were "millionaires-in-waiting." True to our dream, we discovered, in the most unlikely of places, a home show, the product we were sure would make us rich and famous, change our lives forever, and the way products would forever be sold on TV.

Ed

As our friendship grew, I told Barry about an idea that had been bouncing around in my head. As an account executive with the NBC television station in Rhode Island, I started to think about all the record offers that were on the air. They were selling like hotcakes! I knew they had limited appeal because someone who liked rock didn't like country, and not everyone wanted to buy Elvis's greatest hits even though it had sold more than a million copies.

I told Barry that if we could find a product that has more universal appeal than a record offer and advertise it in the same TV format, we could create unlimited demand, lots of money, brand recognition, and lots of money. Did I say lots of money?

If They Say It Can't Be Done...

At that point, all we needed was a product. Barry stumbled upon it at a home show. His wife was after him to paint the ceilings in his kitchen and bathroom. Barry, never the domesticated one, couldn't bear the thought of all the paint dripping on his head as he painted his swirled ceilings. While walking through the home show, bored as can be, he saw a guy painting a ceiling with something attached to the end of a broomstick. It wasn't dripping at all and, although the ceiling he was painting was swirled with all those little "stalactites" hanging down, the device he was using was covering everything in one swipe. The pitchman claimed you could paint an entire room in just half an hour with no drips. Barry was sold, and he forked over $10 instantly. The painters were flying out of the building faster than Viagra at a senior citizens' convention.

Now, Barry's not the handiest guy I've ever known. In fact, Home Depot made him the first name on its "do not call" list. But he went home so excited that he painted his ceiling that day. His wife almost fainted. Because it was a "miracle" that Barry actually used the product, we decided to call it the "Miracle Painter." Prior to that, the only thing he'd ever dipped a brush into was barbeque sauce at a backyard cookout. When he told me how great it worked, I knew this was the product we needed.

We decided to start our own company and ingeniously used the first three letters of my last name and the first two of Barry's. Valer Industries was born. Using the back of Barry's transmission shop as "worldwide headquarters" for our new company, we called the product's manufacturer in England and convinced them to give us exclusive marketing rights in the United States. This was quite an achievement given the fact that a hot dog stand was more high-tech than our office was. Not only did we have to maneuver around old transmissions on the floor and oil all over the place, but we had to time our calls to England so the mechanics were not using the loud hydraulic machines.

Barry

Now that we had sewn up the rights to market this fabulous product, we proceeded to focus in on Ed's contacts in the mail-order business in New York. We were convinced we could get them to see this product as a way to expand their businesses beyond record offers. For purposes of background, Ed had been calling on a number of the mail-order firms in New York and could get in to see any one of them, fast.

We pounded the pavement in search of one of the New York advertising agencies that Ed knew who would handle the project. We figured if we could get a small royalty of 50 cents, we could keep our present jobs and split a few hundred thousand dollars if the product was successful.

Ed

The search left us looking so worn out and dejected that panhandlers on the street started giving us money. While everyone said, "Ed, great to see you," we were told repeatedly that "it couldn't be done." We knew they were wrong. We knew we were right. But what could we do? Determined to realize our idea, we took the mission on ourselves. Of course, there was historical precedent. We knew that Noah's Ark was built by amateurs and the *Titanic* was built by experts. We ignored the experts, so we wrote and produced our first TV commercial. Not that we knew anything about how to write and produce a TV commercial. All we knew about ads was that beer commercials ran during football games, and feminine hygiene products ran during soap operas, and you'd better not get the two mixed up. The challenge in making the commercial was to condense the home show demonstration into two minutes and make the viewers as willing to part with their money from a TV commercial as easily as they did at the home show.

Barry

The commercial would become one of our trademark classics. The announcer said, "This man is painting a swirl ceiling in a tuxedo; there's no drip or splatter. He's using the amazing Miracle Painter." What better way to illustrate no drip! In an effort to break through the clutter and grab the attention of the viewer, we created the "grease copy approach." The idea was to grab the viewer in the first few seconds with something dramatic that slides them into the rest of the commercial. We had just created a commercial style that Madison Avenue would endlessly imitate. Well, they called it imitating. We call it stealing. Now that we had the commercial, we needed to get it on the air and test it. Ed's working at a TV station sure made that convenient. The results were amazing!

Ed

Soon Barry's garage at home was converted into the office, warehouse, and distribution center for the Miracle Painter, and checks from all over America began to pour in. Some of the more famous checks we received came from the Russian Embassy, and others from celebrities, including John Wayne and Raquel Welch. We never cashed these celebrity checks and secretly hoped that one day we would become famous enough that people would not cash our checks either. We are still waiting.

We, assisted by our wives, deposited checks, typed mailing labels, and mailed out products eight to 10 hours a day, while still retaining our full-time jobs: mine in TV and Barry at his AAMCO Transmission franchise. As sales increased, we even used Boeing 747s to fly the Miracle Painters over from England.

Barry

Total Miracle Painter sales: $10 million on one million units sold. We felt so rich that we wouldn't even take calls from Donald Trump. Ed went out and bought a new car, parked it in front of the TV station where he was still employed—in the owner's parking space—then went inside and started cleaning out his desk. The boss saw him and asked what he was doing. Ed said, "I quit." He wanted to know why. Ed said, "I just sold a million Mircale Painters."

His boss thought about it, then took a deep breath and said (sarcastically), "You know, if you don't want to tell me, just say so."

Ed

I had no desire to stay and work for someone else. My philosophy was, "Anytime you sell a million of anything, you're in business."

The Wisdom of Ginsu

As Mark Twain once said, "All you need in this life is ignorance and confidence, and then success is assured." That was us, all right. At the time, we weren't smart enough to realize that it was absurd to expect we could market a product that would sell in the millions. Only later, when we were older and wiser, did we know enough to realize what we had done came more from the optimism of youth than conventional wisdom. We were blindly confident, ignoring convention, blazing our own path, and that's how we succeeded.

As far as doing it ourselves, that was fine with me. After all, there's no way you can sit on your assets and slide uphill.

Barry

Madison Avenue's ignorance combined with our confidence provided us with the greatest opportunity of our lives. Some people just don't know enough to know that they don't know. Imagine if we had listened to the experts. They say that good things come to those who wait. We say, only what's left over, from those who hustle!

Remember, "if they say it can't be done, that means you'll just have to do it yourself!"

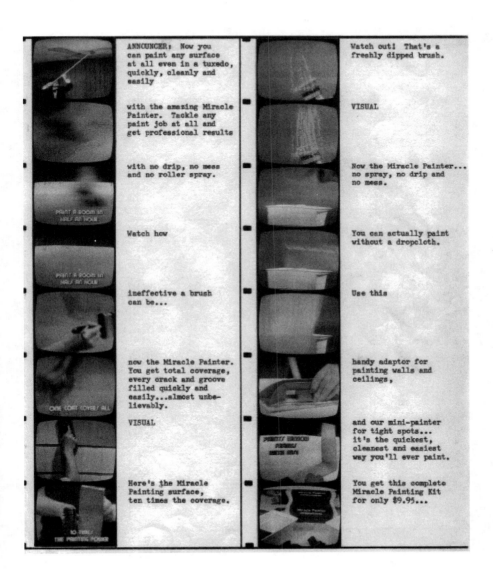

ANNOUNCER: Now you can paint any surface at all even in a tuxedo, quickly, cleanly and easily

with the amazing Miracle Painter. Tackle any paint job at all and get professional results

with no drip, no mess and no roller spray.

Watch how

ineffective a brush can be...

now the Miracle Painter. You get total coverage, every crack and groove filled quickly and easily...almost unbelievably.

VISUAL

Here's the Miracle Painting surface, ten times the coverage.

Watch out! That's a freshly dipped brush.

VISUAL

Now the Miracle Painter... no spray, no drip and no mess.

You can actually paint without a dropcloth.

Use this

handy adaptor for painting walls and ceilings,

and our mini-painter for tight spots... it's the quickest, cleanest and easiest way you'll ever paint.

You get this complete Miracle Painting Kit for only $9.95...

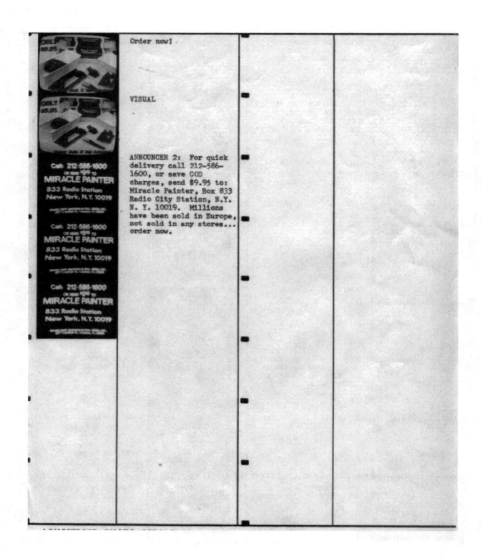

Order now!

VISUAL

ANNOUNCER 2: For quick
delivery call 212-586-
1600, or save COD
charges, send $9.95 to:
Miracle Painter, Box 833
Radio City Station, N.Y.
N. Y. 10019. Millions
have been sold in Europe,
not sold in any stores...
order now.

People Believe What They See and See What They Believe

Ed

In the movie *Catch Me If You Can* (a true story), Leonardo DiCaprio portrayed a man who got away with just about everything by understanding this Ginsuism. By assuming the disguise of a Pan Am airline pilot, he was able to fly around the globe for free and cash phony payroll checks. Now, we're not endorsing a life of crime, but there are ways to help people believe what they see and to accept what you are saying as gospel. I remember when my youngest daughter applied to MIT. One evening we were invited to an information session about the school where they try to convince you that it's the best college to attend. Part of the presentation was to watch a 10-minute video. It was created to be funny and to take the serious edge off the school. In other words, not only eggheads apply. One part of the film especially caught my attention. They were talking, in a lighthearted way, about what you could do with a degree from MIT. One of the things they said you could do, apart from getting rich, marrying the person of your dreams, and living in a Beverly Hills mansion, was "you can get up in front of any group, speak about any subject, have it all be untrue, and everyone will believe you." They were kidding, of course, but it was still insightful. People want to believe!

When we first contacted the English manufacturers of our first product (Miracle Painter) they mentioned that they had business in the United States and they would be coming to New York in a few weeks. We told them we would be happy to meet then in New York at Kennedy Airport. On the appointed day, we met in a restaurant in the terminal. They sure were interesting guys. Phil was about 6 feet tall, slender, and dressed like he just stepped out of *GQ* magazine. His hands were manicured. He looked like he could play James Bond in the next Bond movie, and he spoke the King's English. He reeked of royalty. Mickey was shorter, had an Afro hairstyle, and spoke in a heavy English Cockney accent, like Eliza Doolittle in *My Fair Lady*. It was difficult to understand anything he said, especially when he started to speak in Cockney rhyming slang. The origins of Cockney rhyming slang are uncertain. Some stories say that this slang originated in the market place so that the vendor's could communicate without the customers knowing what was being said. Other stories have it that it originated in the prisons so that inmates could talk without the guards listening in. It doesn't really matter where it comes from; the important thing is that it exists today just as it has for many, many years and can provide a wonderful, colorful language in everyday life. An example of this slang is:

"Got to my mickey, found me way up the apples, put on me whistle and the bloody dog went. It was me trouble telling me to fetch the teapots."

Which really means:

"Got to my house (mickey mouse), found my way up the stairs (apples and pears), put on my suit (whistle and flute) when the phone (dog and bone) rang. It was my wife (trouble and strife) telling me to get the kids (teapot lids)."

Well, towards the end of our meeting Phil and Mickey mentioned that before returning to England they would like to see our office facilities. Oops. You see, we had told them that we were a large marketing company, and little did they know we hadn't ever marketed anything and we were hoping that their painting device would be our first product. We had a dilemma. They told us that they would come to our Rhode Island offices in a week.

We had no office, just the previously mentioned transmission shop. Panic-stricken, we managed to finish our meal without choking and tried to remain and look calm over the possibility of our entire plan being discovered. On the plane trip back, what to do consumed the entire flight time home. Determined to impress the Brits, and keep our reputations intact, we came upon a brilliant idea. We would rent a beautiful office suite in a high-rise tower for the day and pretended that it was our world headquarters. When the Brits arrived that day, we took them on a tour. A tour? Heck, we didn't even know where the men's room was. We'd pass a secretary in the hall, and say, "Make sure that memo to our legal department goes out today, Miss Jones." She had no idea who we were or what we were talking about. She worked in another office down the hall. The closest thing we had to a legal department were the 8 1/2 x 11 legal pads we had in our briefcases. It must have worked, though, because they signed on with us and gave us U.S. exclusivity.

Later, our attorney wanted us to visit their factory in Manchester, England, to make sure that they were indeed the owners of the product and capable of manufacturing the painter. At the time we were both still working our full-time jobs, so we hired an unemployed friend to go to England for us. We told him that these English people were very important to us and that they manufactured the paint pad device that we were interested in purchasing. Our friend came back from Manchester with a glowing report. He told us that they had a huge factory and many thousands of painters in stock. He was very impressed with their facility.

Some years later, we confessed our little ruse to the Englishmen only to discover that the Brits had done the same thing to us. On the day of our friend's visit to England, they had rented an enormous factory for a day to impress us and moved some of their last inventory into the factory to make it look like it was being manufactured there.

Can you believe it? You just can't trust anybody!

When they came to Rhode Island, they saw what they wanted to see. When we sent our representative to England, he saw what he wanted to see.

This Ginsuism crosses over into everyday life, too. Most people start out wanting to believe in you and anything you say. Then the trust is yours to lose. Unfortunately, we give people too many reasons not to believe in us because of negative statements we make and the attitude we project. Because people think with their eyes and ears, you can change the way people think about you by always projecting a positive attitude. Get excited and show it! As famous football coach Vince Lombardi said, "If you aren't fired up with enthusiasm, you will be fired with enthusiasm...by me!" Eliminate words from your vocabulary that contribute to doubt, such as, "I'm not sure," "I can't do that," or "I don't know." Why would you give someone an answer before checking? Some people are on autopilot when it comes to these words. It's okay to be unsure, just express it differently and positively, such as, "I'll get right back to you," or "I'll look into it." Doesn't that sound more positive? Remember that making statements that suggest you are unsure of yourself, or don't believe in yourself, puts doubt in the minds of the people that you are trying to sell to, or impress with your ideas.

If you can *see it*, you can *be it*. It all begins with faith and confidence in yourself that you simply pass on to others who want to believe in you, your product, or what they think they see.

Remember, not everything is as it seems and "people believe what they see and see what they believe."

Zig When Other People Zag

Ed

I'm not sure where the word *zig* comes from but I think our English partners used it often. It was meant to imply "good move." In business and in life we are all faced with decisions. Forks in the road, so to speak. Just as we always do, you should try to train your mind to look for the zig, the alternate way of doing something. Whether overcoming obstacles or making a decision, many times there are options. You just have to look for them. Our entire careers were, and continue to be, based on looking for the zig. I seriously doubt that if we followed the traditional way of doing business we would have ever come up with Ginsu, let alone be in this business at all. Logic dictated that the television direct

39

response business was all about record offers, not products. Therefore, we should have avoided selling products entirely, especially products such as cookware and painters.

As Mr. Spock of *Star Trek* said repeatedly, "Logic dictates."

Logic dictated that we should have stayed out of the knife business. With so many knife offers on TV and with everyone having a drawerful, how could we make money? We did all of these things and more because we zigged when everyone else said we should have zagged. If you think about your life and the decisions you have made, perhaps there was an opportunity for you that you may have passed up because your thinking was one-dimensional. I believe there are always alternatives. They are, however, not always visible. Learning to think differently will make them appear. It's truly amazing. Try it, it works.

Here's a simplistic story, but the point is well made. I remember my first trip to Disney World. Because I had never been there before, naturally I was intimidated by its vastness and worried about the lines. I remember reading in a book from an expert on the park that the shortest times in lines were possible if you always pick the lines on the right (many rides have two or more lines feeding into a ride). Why? He wrote that for some unknown reason people tend to always go to the left when given a choice of two lines. Therefore, the right line moves faster into the ride. I tried it, and it works. Wow, I thought, what a zig! Here's another really good one.

Barry

We were nearing the end of our first year in business and we had pumped up Miracle Painter sales to 20,000 sets per week. We felt enormously successful taking in $200,000 a week. We were on top of the world and only foreseeing better things to come. Then disaster struck: United Parcel Service (UPS) went on strike!

Now, back in the 1970s, things were a little different than they are today. Actually, they were a lot different. You see, the credit card and 800-number system we are so accustomed to using today were just in their infancy back then. The use of 800 numbers had just started, and most people didn't believe that the call was really free. How could monopoly AT&T (at that time it was the only telephone company in the country) not charge you for a call? "They must be sneaking it into your phone bill somewhere," said my friends. I must admit that I was suspicious, too, until I found out that the call was paid for by the receiving party. However, a great portion of America was suspicious of 800 numbers and wouldn't call one. What's more, most people felt more comfortable calling a local number to order. It gave them the confidence that they would indeed receive the product and that the offer was legitimate. Life sure would have been easier for us if everyone trusted the phone company, but because they didn't, we had to set up local answering services with local phone numbers in every city that we ran our commercials in.

Furthermore, because there was no method of taking credit card orders over the phone, if a person wanted to order a Miracle Painter, he would either have to mail a check or order it COD. In the beginning about 90 percent of the people ordered COD, so our method of shipping was with UPS. United Parcel would (and so would we) add a fee for handling a COD order and attempt delivery of the product three times. If UPS could not deliver it and get the money, the company would return the product to us. Of course, we had to pay UPS for shipping and COD charges even if UPS didn't deliver the product and collect the money. This occurred about 10 percent of the time with the Miracle Painter. After UPS collected the money it still took about three weeks to forward it to us. You can start to see that a lot of our money was constantly held up in transit. We were getting about 20,000 orders a week, so 18,000 were probably CODs, and after three weeks, UPS owed us about $600,000. That's a lot of money now, but back in the 1970s you could practically buy a new Learjet for that kind of money.

So there we were, shipping 90 percent of our orders through UPS and *wham*, the drivers go on strike with hundreds of thousands of dollars of our product and money stuck in their system. What was even worse was the fact that we no longer had a method of shipping 90 percent of our orders. If the strike went on too long, we would be in serious trouble, perhaps out of business.

Now, you have to remember there was no low-cost alternative to UPS at that time. There was Railway Express and the post office. Oh yes, I think it was about that time some company named FedEx was starting an overnight delivery service, but it was expensive. FedEx charged more to deliver a letter over night than we did for the whole Miracle Painter. Anyway, we had a serious problem on our hands and it was time to look for a *zig*.

It seemed as though our only alternative was to use the post office. The problem with the post office was that it charged more than UPS for a 1-pound package and postal carriers couldn't accept cash on CODs. The package recipient would have to go get a money order and wait for the postman to show up a second time with his package. If the post office was at an inconvenient location or the person didn't have the time to go and get a money order, we would lose the sale.

Well, it seemed as if we didn't have any choice. We could hold off shipping for a week or two, but then we would have to use the good old U.S. government post office.

Now, in my research to find an alternative method of shipping our product, I understood that I absolutely needed to *zig*. After many meetings with the post office officials, I determined a number of things. One was that our product weighed 1 pound 3 ounces in its heavy cardboard sleeve. Two, if it weighed less than a pound and we could put together 100 units to the same zip codes, it would qualify for bulk rate shipping. The post office's normal rate was $1.09 per pound. We were paying 90 cents with UPS. If the product weighed 15.99 ounces, it would cost us only 18 cents to ship at the bulk mail rate. This was shaping up to be a good zig!

If there was any way to get our product down to 15.99 ounces, I was going to find it! I immediately called Mickey and Phil (the manufacturers) in England and told them we had to get rid of the sleeve on the product and find something lighter. Realizing that the phenomenal sales of their product could be coming to an end because of the strike, they jumped on a plane and flew over. They tried thinner cardboard. It didn't work! It was too heavy! So they tried even thinner cardboard. Didn't work! Too heavy! So they figured what the hell, let's try paper. Two problems: the paper ripped easily and everything fell out—also, too heavy! We were in serious trouble.

I don't know if it was Mickey, Phil, or me, but one of us suggested a plastic wrap. They went out and had the Miracle Painter wrapped in thick plastic. The next weigh-in was at 16.1 ounces. Was it possible to use even thinner plastic? We only needed an ounce. They went out, and a day later returned with it shrink-wrapped in ultra-thin flimsy plastic.

During this whole time I was constantly going over to my friend's business to weigh the Miracle Painter. My friend Bill was in the business of melting down precious jewelry and separating the contents into gold, silver, platinum, and so on. Bill had the most accurate scales I had ever seen, and he was kind enough to let me use his equipment. I brought to his office the Miracle Painter shrink-wrapped in ultra-thin plastic and asked him to weigh it. He said, "Barry, you are a pain in the ass," but here it goes. "It's 15.98 ounces!" he yelled. I grabbed it, gave him a big hug, and ran out of there. Next stop was the post office, where I was hoping it would meet their packing approval. After banging it around a bit they weighed it on three different scales and then gave me a thumbs-up. Yes!

We now had a way to ship the product without UPS. Or so I thought. When I explained to post office personnel that I wanted to ship bulk mail COD they said there was no such thing. We could ship our prepaid orders bulk mail and save 72 cents on every order, but a COD was still a COD and we would have to use the regular system.

Well, I guess we didn't make a full zig out of the scenario, but it counts for half a zig. Well, wait a minute. We still sold about another 300,000 Miracle Painters, and the prepaid to COD ratio changed for the better the more we advertised. It seemed that the more the customers saw our commercial, the more confidence they had that we were indeed legitimate and would ship them the product, so we started to receive a much higher percentage of prepaid orders. We ended up selling about 140,000 additional prepaid orders, so the savings in shipping was about $100,000, which went right to the bottom line. I think that that qualifies for a zig!

We still had a lot of work to do. As two weeks had already gone by, there appeared to be no doubt that we would have to use the post office for CODs. We prepared immediately for the switch over and within days our CODs were going out through the U.S. postal system.

A month went by and we were getting our first results from our initial shipment through the post office. The results were dismal. It was apparent that COD delivery by the post office was going to be a failure. If the person wasn't home, the mail carrier would leave one of those little papers saying that the product would be held at the post office for a while and our customer had to go to the post office and pick up the product themselves. It was obvious that the customers weren't doing that about 50 percent of the time. UPS had been delivering more than 90 percent of our CODs! We were suddenly 40 percent of our income. The pressure was unbelievable. I felt like I was holding the whole world over my head, and it sure was getting heavy.

Now, I'm the type of person who reads the newspaper from beginning to end every morning, and one morning I was reading an article about the strike, and at the end of the article it said, "...and it looks like the strike will continue east of Chicago." I almost fell out of my chair when I read that. What was this east of Chicago thing? As soon as I got to the office I called the management office at UPS and asked, "What is this East Chicago thing?" They informed me that the strike was only in the eastern region. I asked why on earth they hadn't told me that before and the reply was, "It wouldn't matter. You would have to bring your product to Chicago for it to be shipped, so we didn't tell you." I was starting to feel that UPS really didn't appreciate our business. In the years to come I would find that that was really an understatement. Here we were, giving them $30,000 to $40,000 a week in business, and UPS didn't even tell us all the details of the strike. Was there a way we could zig in this situation? What if we loaded up trucks with the Miracle Painters and sent them to Chicago? How many would fit in a truck? What would it cost to get that truck to Chicago?

The results were astonishing! We could hire a trucking company, load the truck with Miracle Painters, deliver them to the UPS loading dock in Chicago, and have UPS ship to our customers in Chicago and every state west of Illinois for about the same money it was costing us to ship through the post office. At that time we were getting about 50 percent of our orders from Illinois and the western part of the country, so we had to make this shipping change immediately. Then UPS threw us another curve. UPS said it could give us a Chicago shipper number, but we had to have a local address where the undeliverable painters could be returned. We sure didn't have an office in Chicago, so I relied on the old pals act once again. My friends Lew and Fern, who I had grown up with, had recently moved to Chicago. I called them up and asked them if they would accept the undeliverable product for me in their garage.

They were happy to help and replied, "Sure, why not."

I don't think they or I knew what they were getting into. You see we were selling about 8,000 COD painters a week from Chicago and west of there. UPS delivered about 90 percent, so that means that 10 percent, or 800 units, of product came back to their house every week.

After a few weeks Fern called me in a panic, saying, "We have so many painters in my garage that I can barely close the door! Please get them out of here! I feel like I am being attacked by Miracle Painters!"

Now it was the situation in reverse. We had to find a trucker to go to their house, pick up the product, and bring it back to us so we could repack it and ship it out again. Once that was accomplished, our crisis was at least half over. Now that's a zig!

A couple of months later the strike ended and everything returned to normal. At least we thought it did. You see, we decided to meet with K-Tel International (more on this later) about having them sell the Miracle Painter in Europe. So on December 16, 1976, I took an American Airlines flight to Chicago with the intent of catching a connection to Manitoba, Canada, where the K-Tel offices were located. A few days before the flight I had been watching a TV program called "Terror at 30,000 Feet" in which an elderly police officer is escorting a prisoner on a flight. The detective in the film starts getting pains in his left arm and suffers a massive heart attack, and the convict takes over the plane. Now here I am at 30,000 feet and I start to get strange feelings in my left arm. I was 35 years old at the time and I figured I couldn't be having a heart attack, but I panicked a little because I had just seen that movie. It's a good thing I did panic. I told the flight attendant of my problem and she quickly made an announcement asking if there was a doctor on board. There wasn't, but a nurse showed up and was concerned about me. They asked if I thought I could continue on to Chicago and I felt that I could. When we landed in Chicago an EMT squad immediately got on the plane and started all sorts of medical procedures including performing an EKG, taking my blood pressure, and even starting an IV. Now I was really getting concerned. As the male passengers were getting off the plane they were looking at me as if I was a freak. The females had sympathy and concern in their eyes. They took me by ambulance to Resurrection Hospital, which served O'Hare Airport, and I ended up in intensive care with a heart attack. My day trip to Manitoba turned into a seven-day hospital stay in Chicago.

Let me tell you, that was an eye-opener. I previously told you that I felt that I was holding the whole world over my head during our time of crisis. Well, after the strike ended I still felt that way, but I guess I thought it was okay to wipe the sweat off my brow. When I did that, the whole world came crashing down on me and I had the heart attack. Ed and I had been smoking two packs of cigarettes a day in our offices. That day was the last time I ever smoked anything, and within a year Ed had quit also.

Now it was time for another zig. Within four weeks I was back at the grind brainstorming our next product with the guys and doing all the other things necessary to ensure the success of the company.

As I write this I am 63 years old, so I guess the zigs I made over the last 28 years were good ones.

It's difficult to teach people to zig. Hopefully this story will serve as inspiration for you to start thinking in the same way we do. Don't be thrown off your game when others zag. Concentrate on the situation and find a good zig to get you through. We have said and will say again throughout this book about the importance of training your mind to think differently. Picking a man to demonstrate the Miracle Painter in a tuxedo instead of just a regular guy on a ladder is a good zig, picking a Japanese name for a knife that came from Ohio is a good zig.

Think you can't think this way? Think again. Just resist going down the traditional road. No matter how crazy it sounds at first, keep doing it over and over again on everything you do. Eventually it will be second nature to you and you will have learned to zig.

So, remember: Don't always follow the crowd; follow your own instincts and unique way of doing things. Experiment, diversify, dare to take calculated risks on a regular basis. In other words, "always *zig* when other people zag."

Always Ask

Ed

Remember when you were in high school? I know I do. In every school there was always this one great-looking girl who everyone wanted to date. We would dream about her nightly and wanted to ask her out but always thought, "She'll never go out with me." Every other boy in school was probably thinking the same thing. But no matter how much we wanted to date her, we wouldn't dare ask her out. We just knew that she would turn us down. How could we face that kind of rejection?

She would probably laugh and say, "Are you kidding, or what?"

Guess what? One day she's with this one ordinary-looking guy and you say, "How does a guy like that get her?" The answer is, he was the only one who had the guts to ask her out!

I remember watching a television show where they were interviewing this beautiful model. The host asked, "Tell me, did you date much in school?"

She replied, " No, no one ever asked me out. They were afraid I would say no. Actually, if they did ask I would have said *yes!*"

It's too late now, and we can't go back in a time machine, but you can increase your chances going forward by asking.

The rule of "Always Ask" and believing that anything can be negotiated works for just about everything. We like to say, "If it's free, it's for me!" Wherever we shop we negotiate. Where? Try it at the places you buy clothes. It's not uncommon for me to get a free shirt or tie when I buy a suit. Ask; someone might say yes. Not asking is an automatic no.

Cars, hotels, airlines, shoes, you name it. When I fly, I routinely ask if any seats are open in first class. I explain what a good customer I am and would appreciate a "bump up." Does it work? Sometimes. Don't ask, and you sit in coach. Remember that the most anyone can say is no! Are you a full-time student or part-time continuing education student? If you received anything less than the grade you were expecting, try asking your instructor or professor for a better grade and be prepared to explain why you feel you deserved more. Most students who think they deserved a better grade just go away. Big mistake. Ask! What if she says yes? She could say, "Why don't you try a rewrite and give it back to me?" Opportunity!

Want that promotion? Ask for it. You may find that your boss was waiting all along for you to ask as a demonstration of your desire for the position.

Same goes for a raise. Why is it that when it comes to asking for deals, car dealers, flea markets, and home purchases are the areas we feel most comfortable asking about? Everything else is taboo.

You would never think of asking for a deal at Saks, right? Wrong. I have asked and received discounts at some of the most prestigious stores. Ask. I'm sure if you think about it you'll find many opportunities to ask and negotiate something better for yourself.

Barry

Negotiating is both an art form and a science. One tactic I've used many times is to ask for 20 things in a contract when I really only want two or three. I know if I asked for only two or three things that I really wanted, the other side would analyze them to death and try to give me only one. Asking for 20 things gives me something to give up and still make sure that I get what I want. If someone asks you how much you are willing to pay for an item, say, "I want it for free!" Whatever price they were thinking of asking will be immediately lowered. If you are entering a business deal and you are asked what percentage you want to enter the deal, say, "90 percent." After you see the look of shock in their eyes, you'll know that whatever they were originally thinking of giving you has now been raised by quite a few percentage points.

Ask! I'm sure if you think about it, you'll find many opportunities to ask and negotiate something better for yourself and keep some extra money in your pocket.

Ed

Barry and I once figured out how much money we had saved over a lifetime by simply asking. It was more than a million dollars. I cannot think of any situation in life that this Ginsuism does not apply to. I am never embarrassed by asking and don't spend a lot of time thinking about what someone would think of me for asking. In fact, I find just the opposite. I find many people admire and respect my ability and consider me a good businessperson.

There was an old woman who used to sell pretzels outside an office building in New York City. A young executive felt sorry for her, so every day he'd put down a quarter and not take a pretzel. One day she said, "Excuse me sir, may I have a word with you?"

He said, "You're going to ask me why I give you a quarter every day and don't take a pretzel?"

She said, "No. I wanted to tell you that the price is now 50 cents."

Just as the pretzel lady was not afraid to ask, neither should you be. We certainly weren't. In fact, I recall that in 1975 when we were first purchasing TV time on stations all over the country to support our first product, the Miracle Painter, we used to ask every station we ran on for extra spots to help improve our profit margins.

Our profit on the item varied because the advertising cost to get an order for the product was different in every state, on every TV station, and in every show! Here's how it worked. The price of every-thing except advertising was a fixed cost. Fixed costs consisted of the price of the product, answering services, packaging, fulfillment, post-age, telephone costs, and overhead. The difference between all of those fixed costs and the selling price was all that we could spend on adver-tising to get an order. As an example, let's say our fixed cost was $5. A sale price of $10 left us $5 for advertising. If the advertising cost per order came in over the $5, we were in trouble. So we watched that advertising cost on every station on a daily basis. It was exacting and tedious. We would have to call every station to ask if any checks had come in to the station for the Miracle Painter. They would tell us how many envelopes they had received. Then we would call the answering service that we used in that market and find out how many COD calls we had received. Then we had to call our salesperson and ask him how many spots had run the day before and also their cost. When we finally had all that information it was easy to divide the cost of the TV spots by the amount of orders and get a CPO (cost per order). If it was too high, we would have to cancel the station. If it was okay, we would let it ride. If it was very low, we would order more time on the station. We looked at all TV stations as if they were retail stores. If they weren't profitable, we closed them instantly. At times, if a sta-tion was at a break-even point, we might rearrange the schedule to give it a fresh approach, ask for some free air time, or try to negotiate a lower price.

Most people would never think that direct response television time is negotiable. Well, it is! It was interesting to see what salespeople would do if we told them when we were losing money. Invariably, they would offer us free spots to bring down our cost per order. If we felt that wasn't enough, they would also lower the cost of the spots. Our philosophy at that time was simple. What if we could get a $1,000 spot for $500? What if we could get it for $500 and get one additional spot free? How about two free? Could we give a six-week commitment and get even more free? Sure we could! We asked everyone for free air time to run our commercials. Most everyone said yes! We asked them for two-for-one deals. They said yes! We asked for the stars and usually got them. We were now cutting the advertising cost per order in half or better. The profits kept rising as our advertising costs went down.

We even asked our customers for more. When the commercials were ready to air, we always tested two things: the offer and the price. For example, we would test three markets at $19.95 and three at $29.95. Sometimes prices were raised because the offer was perceived to be too inexpensive or simply because we "asked" for more. Those were the markets we loved: people who wanted to spend more and get less. And they didn't all work for the government, either.

You'll find that if you remember to use this Ginsuism, many people will say yes!

So, remember: No guts, no glory. The worst anyone can possibly say is no, so "always ask!"

If Your PartnerShip
Starts to Sink

Down dooby doo down down
Breaking up is hard to do

—"Breaking up Is Hard to Do," Neil Sedaka

Barry

Nobody ever goes into any type of relationship expecting the worst. In fact, in most partnerships you're either both pretty much thinking "forever" or at least one of you is while the other is thinking "for quite a while!" Statistics tell us that just over 50 percent of all marriages are doomed to failure, and the numbers are much greater than that for business partnerships and/or businesses that fail. The funny thing is, I'd have to say that 100 percent of us entering these partnerships, both personal and professional, don't think that we're ever going to be part of the 50 percent or more that fail. Yet, I've had it happen to me twice in business and once in marriage; so, I would be the first to tell you…it can happen to anyone. What's more, until things really started to go bad, I never really saw it coming and hoped until the end that it would go back to the way it once was. But it didn't, and learning to accept that and move on was one of the hardest lessons I have ever had to learn. It's much easier, if you never cared about someone, to just up and leave. But when the partnership has been a good one and it goes bad, the emotional baggage you carry out of it can weigh you down for lifetime…if you let it.

The tale of "a good partnership gone bad" is an all too familiar one. You aren't the first person it's happened to, and you definitely won't be the last. Could you (or your partner) have prevented it? You know, I'm pretty sure in the case of any type of partnership that fails, that eventually it would have failed anyway for reasons that are often hard to control. They range from philosophical differences and growing apart to selfishness, unwillingness to compromise, and irresponsibility. But in the case of long-term relationships that continue to work, there are definitely things you can do and point to that help keep that relationship going strong. For example, with Ed and I there were quite a few rough moments over 30 years, but as we've jokingly said before, the reason that we have had a successful partnership for 30 years is "we have never had sex together."

What I'm trying to say is, we've never screwed each other—literally or figuratively! No matter how difficult a decision we were faced with or what type of situation or question came up, we always made sure that we had each other's best interests at heart.

Sometimes, we don't see things exactly the same way, but we hash it out and refuse to let our differences get in the way of our friendship. We respect each other and our respective families. We choose our battles carefully and try not to say anything that might offend the other. And like any old married couple, deep down we both know that we still love each other.

My theory on why partnerships and marriages get into trouble is this: When a marriage or partnership takes place, I picture a beautiful statue being created of the two people involved. Every time something goes wrong and someone says something negative that can't be taken back, it is like taking a chisel and hammer and chipping out a piece of the statue. A small remark chisels off a finger or an earlobe. A more serious remark takes off a hand or kneecap. Over the years the statue starts to crumble and the final problem between the two people causes the statue to fall and the relationship to fail.

Ed

And the similarities between why matrimonial and business partnerships break up, and stay intact, don't end there. In fact, if you really think about it, a lot of the reasons couples break up are the same reasons business partnerships don't work out as well. Let me elaborate on what I mean by listing a few of the more common reasons:

1. **Money.** How does a partnership fail because of money? Simple, in the same ways and for the same reasons that marriages go bad over money. Think about it: Some partners have as much at stake in their business as they do in their marriage, and spend nearly as much time with each other as they do with their spouses…if not more! Money certainly can be a crowbar in a relationship. How? If one partner starts making money decisions that are not agreed on by all partners, spends money carelessly, doesn't keep track of money properly, doesn't manage the company cash flow, keeps poor or no financial records, keeps financial "secrets" from the other partner (s), and so on. And of course there's always the number-one reason that partnerships fail, related to money: not making enough!

2. **Incompatibility/Irreconcilable Differences.** Things are okay at first, but as time goes by it becomes clear that you have different values, different approaches, different likes, different dislikes, etc. This just makes it increasingly likely that common situations that are normally

"talked out" between partners become major sources of personal angst and professional agitation: hiring family members, paying salaries that are too high, runaway expenses, high-end leased cars, overindulgent or unexplained restaurant tabs, who gets the biggest office, not coming in on time, leaving early, taking time off, excess vacations, even magazine subscriptions can all become major irritants. Sometimes lower-level employees can be a catalyst to breakups by having one of their favorite partners be the recipient of all the dirt going on in the company and by repeating something one of the partners said, perhaps even out of context. In partnership terms this is roughly akin to pouring gasoline on your partner's desk and tossing a lit match on it.

3. **Jealousy/Growing Apart.** As you get older and time goes by, you both normally start to mature, change, and see things in different ways on issues you used to always agree on. At this point, at least one of you decides that you do not wish to "compromise any longer" and that you are "tired of being the one who always gives in." Once this dynamic is set in motion and both partners begin to buy into it, with one being the resenter/victim and the other playing the offender/beneficiary, or both partners alternating these roles, change is most likely inevitable. If life or financial circumstances (or both) suddenly start to favor one partner more than the other, equal footing is lost and jealousy and its own lifelong partner, resentment, will at least make a fleeting appearance in the relationship, if not take on a starring role. The best hope for resolution here is the jealous partner recognizing jealousy and envy for the nasty little emotions they are, counting his own blessings, being happy for his partner's good fortune, and then getting past it. If this doesn't happen, the relationship and partnership are headed up the creek without a paddle.

4. **Stress/ Miscellaneous.** Non-work–related personal issues combined with things not going well business-wise or in

your professional relationship (all relationships have rough patches) can quickly make working together untenable for both of you, especially if the stress level continues to ratchet upward and you start to lose control and say things that you may not be able to take back later. When a partnership reaches this level, getting off-site, away from the chaos and confusion, and dealing with the high stress personal situation first can quickly deflate this huge hot air balloon and bring both partners back to earth in a hurry before it is too late.

I have to tell you, one of the saddest things you will ever face in business or life is having to walk away from a partner who was once your friend and confidant. Yet, even though I'm all for doing whatever is possible to save a relationship personally or professionally, sometimes, once things cross a certain line, you have no choice but to cut your losses and move on, for both your partner's sake and your own. How do you know when you've reached that point? Well, each person is different, but here are some *universal warning signs* that can signal that any type of relationship may have sprung a leak and is beginning to take on water:

1. Questions you used to get quick and complete answers to no longer get much more response than a barely distinguishable guttural noise.

2. More and more "little things" stop making sense without satisfactory explanations.

3. You are not being included in meetings and calls you used to be included in.

4. There is a continual feeling of uneasiness or tension, and, when you try to discuss it, the discussion goes nowhere.

5. Discussions are cut short when you enter a room and doors are closed for a lot more phone conversations than usual.

6. You start noticing a lot of unexplained absences.

7. There are awkward silences between you, when there never were before.

8. You have no proof, but your gut continually tells you something is wrong.

9. In general, you are spending a lot less time together.

10. You wake up one morning and find a knife in your back.

Only kidding about that last one; most warning signs are not that obvious, until after you have discovered for sure that the ship (be it partner, relation, or friend) is, in fact, sinking. What do you do when you know for sure? Well, you can go down with the ship or you can grab a lifejacket (whatever you can salvage materially and spiritually from the relationship), jump quickly overboard, and start swimming for shore. I know what my choice would be.

And by the way, is it possible that a few of these warning signs could exist at the same time without your partner being guilty of anything? Absolutely, so don't confront your partner and throw away a valuable relationship unless you are absolutely sure that something is really wrong! Your longtime partner deserves the benefit of the doubt...and a chance to explain. You would expect the same!

The lesson here is that partnerships (and all relationships) can go bad for many different reasons, and, when they do, sometimes it's better for the two of you to simply move on rather than waste your time trying to save something that can't be saved.

Which, by the way, is another interesting observation when it comes to running a small business successfully. For some reason, just like in a marriage, two seems to be the magic number that works best. Three is (often) a crowd and four, as far I'm concerned, is almost always a disaster, even if things go very well for a while. Again, there is no scientific reason why, it just seems to be a part of human nature, especially among entrepreneurs: two of them can compromise and agree often enough, but put four strong-willed leaders into the equation and what do you think is going to happen eventually? They pair off into sets of two and do battle! Unfortunately, we learned this Ginsuism the hard way!

Here's what happened to us.

If Your PartnerShip Start to Sink

The Miracle Painter was made in England by the two British blokes we previously mentioned. At first we were their customers, then with a move that I would call "my brain taking a vacation from my body," we made them our partners. What a bad move! Here's why!

First, one of them decided to move to Rhode Island. Then the other one decided that he should move here, too. Then the wives, the kids, the dog, and so on. I guess we should have realized that all along they were interested in making a move to the States. I remember how excited they were to be in the United States and especially how attractive it was for them to return to the UK and say, "I own a company in America."

It was Mickey Walsh who made the first move here with his wife, Estelle. They settled in Rhode Island, and Mickey worked out of our offices while he was busy setting up manufacturing of the painters. In no time at all they had contracted with a nearby plastics company to make the new product, and moved the tooling to the United States. We were thrilled! And why not? Just look at the savings. No freight, no duty, nothing! With the help of our friends and attorneys, Schecter, Abrams and Verri, they had established a foothold in the United States with a Rhode Island corporation, a manufacturing contract with a factory, and good customers to buy the product—us. I would be remiss if I didn't add that all of this went down easily because we genuinely liked these guys quite a bit. Plus, they were incredibly bright and talented. They were with us constantly. We would invite them to join us for every social or family event we had, and they would do likewise. We often ate out together with our wives. We even vacationed together. Plus, they were just great fun to be with, especially Mickey. Everyone took to him. They just loved his accent. He also had a wit about him that kept us laughing all the time.

While Mickey was digging in here, Phil remained in England to establish the UK arm for our company (we were equally excited about saying, "We own a company in England," and started a record company called Valer Records, UK. Again, we used the Valer name with "Val" for Valenti and the "er" for Becher. Phil's first attempt at success was a record compilation called the Black and White Connection, a series of black and white contemporary artists (at the time) such as Lou Rawls; Johnny Nash; Earth, Wind and Fire; ABBA; Peaches and Herb; David Essex; Wild Cherry; Tower of Power; and many more. Phil had managed to have it distributed by Motown Records, UK. He could manage to do just about anything. He was sharp, articulate, and persuasive. The success of the Black and White Connection was moderate at best, but it wasn't until we got into the punk rock music scene that things started to unravel. To this day, I don't know how, but we ended up owning a punk rock band called the Drones. Ever hear of them? That's why it failed. However, back in the old US of A, things were humming.

It was from this vantage point that they launched their next surprise. They said, "Why don't we stay in America, help you develop more products for TV, start a new company, and split the profits four ways?" We agreed, and the new company was called Walshe America, Inc.

We allowed our friendship to cloud our business decisions. We were wearing our friendship glasses.

They had gone from two guys who sold us painters to two guys who were now our partners and were rapidly learning the television marketing business. They were also making quite a bit of money as our partners.

We'd been in business about a year when our British Miracle Painter suppliers told us that they had another product that we might be interested in marketing. It was a portable slicing machine that was made in Germany. Due to the fact that Mickey and Phil had come up with this slicer product, we decided to put the product under Walshe America. Our advertising agency would still be used to market the product, but the profits delivered from the sale of the slicers would be split equally amongst the four of us.

Of course we named this new product the Miracle Slicer and proceeded to make a commercial for it. Mickey knew of a woman in Texas who was an expert with the product, so we flew her to Rhode Island and had her do the demonstrating in the commercial. Next came the testing process, so we aired the commercial on eight TV stations. The test was successful and it looked like we had another winner, so we rolled it out on as many stations as we could. The money started rolling in and kept on rolling in. We all felt that our relationship was working fine and we decided that we should all have separate responsibilities. I was in charge of advertising, Mickey was in charge of new product development, Phil was in charge of procurement and fulfillment (when he was in the country), and Barry was in charge of the finances. Things went along fine for a while and Mickey came up with another product idea we called the Miracle Duster. The duster did fairly well, as we sold about 200,000 of them at $9.95 each.

It was shortly after Mickey came here in 1976 that Elvis Presley died. We had a brilliant idea (or so we thought) that we could sell a line of Elvis Presley jewelry. That idea suffered the same fate as Elvis, and we quickly retreated from the Elvis market. The same thing happened with our *Dogtalk* album, our *Star Wars* jewelry, and our golf swing monitor idea for which we hired golf great Gary Player to appear in the commercial. This was at the same time Phil was in England buying us a punk rock band and producing the Black and White Connection. Money was pouring out of the company faster than shredded documents at Enron.

We had sunk money into a number of projects and none had come to fruition. After a few more years, even though things got better financially, for one reason or another, our relationship started to become unglued and we reenacted the Revolutionary War.

Let me tell you, having to work in an office right next door to someone you hope will soon become your ex-partner is not the most pleasant of experiences. Verbal communication between us and the guys from England stopped quickly, and we started corresponding by memo. It is too bad we didn't have e-mail back then. It sure would have been easier than writing out a memo and giving it to a secretary who proceeded to tell the whole world. If we had taken out a billboard on one of our major highways, less people would have known.

They proceeded to get their own attorney, and then the legal wrangling started. There was always a lurking threat that they would put the company into receivership, but thankfully that never occurred. We needed to make sure that if they decided to take the company down by forcing it into bankruptcy, we would still be able to survive, so we decided to quietly and secretly market a product by ourselves. Here's what we did.

Barry was at a friend's house for dinner one evening when he looked at his knife and fork and noticed that they were from two different sets. He thought that there were probably many sets of flatware such as this and that it might be possible to sell silverware on TV.

He thought that this might be the product we could use to protect our future.

"Do you really think we can sell flatware on TV?" I asked Barry.

"If we can make it look like real silver and give it some magic, we sure can," replied Barry.

Over the next few weeks we worked secretly with our copywriter to develop a pitch and a script. Let's face it, folks, selling silverware to people who don't need it and have no plans to buy it is not an easy thing. Being extremely busy with our legal battle, we had very little time for the flatware project and left most of it, including the filming of the commercial, to our creative department, who flew out to Pittsburgh to film it at a facility we worked with. Creative had come up with an opening for the commercial that had a table set with mismatched flatware and the announcer asking, "Does your silverware look like this? Well it could look like this!" The mismatched pieces then disappeared and were replaced with shiny, matching, beautiful silverware. The commercial then proceeded to extol the virtues of this wonderful flatware that we called Lustreware.

We began thorough testing of the product and found that, with the commercial that had been produced, the product was losing money. The commercial just didn't have what it took to be a winner. We didn't take to the idea of losing money, so we figured we should start paying more attention to Lusterware and less to our legal situation. We realized immediately that the flatware looked a little, well, flat and was not gleaming. We had never really liked the opening of the spot that referred to the mismatched flatware, as we felt the opening wasn't as exciting as our other product openings, Ginsu and Armourcote cookware.

Barry

We decided to spend some serious time on the creative slant of the product. Ed said, "Hmmm, why don't we do something like have a knife thrower and throw one of the knives at a girl like in the circus?"

I said, "Why don't I smash it with a sledgehammer?"

Everyone was wondering what we were smoking.

I said, "Why don't we give it a great guarantee like we did with the Ginsu, you know, 50 years?"

Ed said, "Why don't we guarantee to replace any piece for free, even if you lose it?"

"Fabulous idea, Ed," I replied.

Creative said, "We could use the crazy opening you guys were talking about and when the knife thrower throws the knife at the girl, just before it hits her, we could have it reverse itself into his hand and the announcer say, "Introducing the only silverware you can't throw away!" I replied.

"Or destroy," yelled Ed. "I could use the sledgehammer!"

"It needs something else to go with throwaway and destroy," I replied. "How about if we make a spoon disappear and reappear and say, 'You can't even lose this silverware!'"

We decided to clean up the copy a little and we came up with, "Introducing the only silverware you can't throw away, lose, or destroy. Because if you do, we'll replace it—FREE!"

"I have an old leather vest outfit from my swinging single 1960s days, and I can play the knife thrower," I said.

Ed was into weight lifting at the time, so he volunteered to handle the sledgehammer.

We flew out to Pittsburgh to add the new shots and to re-film the dull silverware shots and make the Lustreware truly *luster ware*.

Of course, something had to go wrong, and it did, when Ed swung the sledgehammer and missed the fork he was trying to hit but broke the table into pieces. We didn't have another table, so we plodded on until the wee hours of the morning until the commercial was finished and, to this day, if you look at the commercial carefully, you can see the fork that Ed missed flying through the air.

Ed

And no, Barry didn't accidentally kill the brave girl who volunteered to be the target for his knife throw. We used a camera angle to make it seem as though he was throwing the knife at her, but he was actually throwing it about 6 feet off to her side. At the end of the commercial we inserted the guarantee, and the announcer read the first line: "If you ever lose a piece, we'll replace it free; if you ever destroy a piece, we'll replace it free. Even if you throw it away, we'll replace it free." In small print on the guarantee it said, "Simply add $1.50 shipping and handling for each piece replaced." That was more than enough to cover all costs. We hurried back to Rhode Island and got the new Lustreware commercial on the air immediately. The result? Twenty million dollars in sales in the next year.

Meanwhile, the Englishmen had never been crazy about living in the northeast with its cold winters, so they were amenable to selling out and moving to the warmer climate of Florida. After what seemed like years, a deal was reached and we agreed to purchase their stock in the various companies in which we were all jointly involved. The price was $400,000.

With friends like that, who needs enemies?

Don't forget this one: Just because a partnership is great when you start it does not mean it is always going to be that way. Sometimes people and partnerships change for any number of reasons. Though there are many things you can and should do to preserve all of the "partnerships" in your life, sometimes the "worm has turned" and the best thing you can do is recognize it and accept it. In short, "if your partner*ship* starts to sink," don't sit there crying, grab a lifejacket and start swimming—and watch out for the sharks!

Keep Your Secrets of Success to Yourself

Barry

When we created our unique style of direct marketing, we wish we'd kept the secrets of our success to ourselves until it was over. We were not in business to educate our competitors. Yet, unwittingly, we did so many times.

If you want to get ahead in this world, keep your secrets of success to yourself. We've all seen movies where someone has a great idea and a coworker or the boss steals it and claims the idea as his or her own. Well, it happens in real life, too.

Remember this: no one who creates something spectacular should ever share it without compensation. Not you! Not us! Not anybody! If you're onto something, develop it, capitalize on it, cash in, and protect it. Then, share it with the world. If you need to feel charitable or have a strong sense of guilt, go volunteer at a hospital. In the movie *Wall Street*, Michael Douglas says, "Greed is good." When it comes to keeping your great ideas or secrets of success to yourself, he's right! Think about this: without greed there is no motivation to be successful. Making money and keeping it is the primary reason you start a business.

In the movie *Star Trek: The Next Generation* when the Starship Enterprise traveled back in time to our present day, a woman from our present time was on board the Starship Enterprise and asked, "How much did it cost to build a ship like this?"

Captain Picard responded, "We don't use money in the 23rd century. We work to better ourselves and humanity."

Great, but until the 23rd century comes around, money is what we use to build Starships, and everything else, today.

And because money is involved and our acknowledged goal is to make, and keep, as much of it as possible, don't expect us to give away any trade secrets. We'll tell you anything you want to know about the mistakes we've made and some of the general business principles and personal relationship approaches we've learned and had success with, but don't expect us to tell you very much about the specific details of our business or industry or particular projects or campaigns, unless we're sure that the information won't help you, let anyone else directly compete with us, or come back to haunt us in any way. If there's any doubt, we err on the side of caution and keep our mouths firmly shut.

Because of this steadfast philosophy, we never cease to be amazed by the incredible number of people in every industry who achieve fabulous results and then can't wait to tell the world exactly how they did it—in trade articles, books, seminars, interviews, restaurants, cocktail parties, you name it.

In our minds, this is like Colonel Sanders or Coca-Cola saying, "Let's release our secret formulas in order to encourage direct competition and stimulate the economy." Yeah, *that'll* happen.

You want to know what gets stimulated when you tell some people your secrets? Their greed, their business, and their profits. The only thing of yours that gets stimulated is your ulcer as you watch your own business go the way of 8-track tapes, typewriters, and the Concorde. Keep it to yourself.

Ever wonder why those "hot" businesses you hear about everywhere one year seem to be struggling or out of business the next? They don't keep their secrets of success to themselves, they don't learn from their past mistakes, and they obviously don't know about Ginsuisms.

By the way, we love the people who can't stop talking about their successes. Thank *you*. Your generosity makes it much easier for the rest of us to make a good living. If you're willing to tell us how to solve difficult problems for free and give away your best ideas for free, then we're definitely open to taking them from you. Into our "swipe file" of stolen ideas they go, ready for the day we need them and most likely use them to take business away from their creators.

No matter how good you are or what level of success you achieve, you're only a human being, so you're going to make mistakes. We didn't keep the secrets of our success close enough, and we spawned several competitors that shouldn't have existed. Here are two quick little anecdotes that show what happened to us and what you don't want to happen to you.

Ed

The first we will call Johnny McVeigh. (He's the one we sent over to inspect the factory in England.) We realized that we couldn't run our fledgling enterprise and continue with our full-time jobs unless we took on another partner. Johnny McVeigh, my friend, was down on his luck and unemployed when we made him an unbelievable offer of 33 percent of our new company for free. Absolutely no cash investment if he would run it full-time. It's unbelievable to us now, but then it was just a third of nothing and futures unknown. Johnny, a barfly, hired untrained cocktail waitresses to become media buyers and secretaries. As soon as the ink was dry, and armed with all of the secrets and wisdom we imparted to him, he started making side deals behind our backs. We were forced to buy him out. Just to prove to you that

The Wisdom of Ginsu

God has a sense of humor, he settled for $20,000 for his 33 percent, a fraction of what it was worth a year later.

As soon as the no-compete on his contract ended, he promptly went into business competing with us. We sure wish we had kept our secrets from him.

Our British partners, who we also ended up buying out, knew absolutely nothing about television marketing when they met us. To be fair, they would argue that we knew next to nothing about demonstrating products until we met them. After months of negotiations, we finally went our separate ways, but we hear that they did very well after their departure with the knowledge we had shared with them. They moved to Florida, and guess what? They entered the direct response business. We definitely should have "screen-tested" these guys better! If we had, we would have saved ourselves a lot of time, money, and heartache!

But our "loose lips sink ships" tendencies didn't stop at Mickey and Phil. Over many lunches, we even told one of our suppliers some of our secrets. He was a trusted individual and we thought he was our friend. One day we heard through the grapevine that he had become a competitor and was vying with us for the same television time to run his own products. Even one of our landlords, who rented us office space, was trying to get in on the action. Apparently, we were considered a cash cow and everyone was lining up to take a drink of "green" milk.

Now, when it comes to employees, should you also adopt this Ginsuism? That's a tough one. Over the years we have employed many people who learned our style of marketing and went on to work for competitors or even start their own businesses. Should we have been more secretive about how we did things? If you are running a business and have good employees, you need to train them for your business to be successful, regardless of the risk. I remember a great line that says it all. It is from a keynote speaker at a seminar I attended.

He asked the audience, "Should you train your employees so that someday they will leave you?"

Many in attendance yelled out no.

70

Keep Your Secrets of Success to Yourself

He went on to say, "Well, what if you don't train them and they stay?" Having employees leave with the knowledge of your business is an inevitable part of being in business. You can, however, avoid some of the problems we had by being more selective and adopting many of the Ginsuisms we detail in this book. It will not stop people from leaving, but it can cut the departures down to a minimum.

Still on the fence about sharing your secrets of success? You won't be after you hear this final tale of woe.

This story falls under the heading of the dumbest thief we ever saw.

We'll never forget the time we were sitting in a restaurant and the guy at the next table was bragging to his lunch guests about how he "screwed the IRS out of a lot of money." He went on to blurt out every little detail on how he had done it. How he wrote off expensive items in his home using company funds. How he wrote off trips for his wife and kids as a business expense. No, he didn't work for Tyco, Enron, or Adelphia. If he said these things any louder, we would have thought he had a microphone. However, we were still amazed that someone would steal and proceed to tell the entire restaurant about it. A few months later we saw a picture of him in the newspaper right under the headlines announcing his indictment. It seems someone in the restaurant was as greedy as he was and turned him into the IRS for the reward.

Ever hear the line "Imitation is the sincerest form of flattery"? Baloney! Be smart and "keep your secrets of success to yourself."

No Problemos

Ed

When I was in the radio business, I had only one way of looking at problems. I refused to recognize they exist. If someone said to me, "Ed, I have a problem," I would always say, "No, you have an opportunity."

No problemos.

Too often we accept something as a problem with no possible resolution, or we create a problem before it actually happens. How many times have you said, "That's it. It's all over," or said, "If this happens, I'm dead!" All of this is worrying before you actually try to develop a solution or worry about a problem that hasn't actually happened. Try looking at problems (real ones, not anticipated ones) as

73

opportunities for you to develop your creative abilities or challenges that require your particular skill set to overcome, or puzzles that only you can solve! In the ad business, creative directors are faced with problems every day; for example, "Find a new slogan for this product that explains the benefits, but use only three words to describe it." Now that's an opportunity! Day after day these people find creative solutions. How? They have brainstorming sessions. They consult others. They even ask their friends and relatives.

Remember, anticipated problems are just that—anticipated problems. It's difficult to find a solution to something that hasn't happened yet, especially when all the possible outcomes are pure speculation on your part, and any time and effort expended on outcomes that don't happen is completely wasted and probably weakened by all the eventualities you had to consider! Worrying will only make you age faster. A real problem is an opportunity for you to find a unique, brilliant, and effective solution. Many times the answers are right in front of you. Look, think, listen, and, most importantly, don't give up! Persistence is just stubbornness with a purpose. If you don't get the answer immediately, let it "marinate" in your brain for a while. You may wake up with the perfect answer in the middle of the night or suddenly realize on the way to work that you know exactly how to solve the problem! What an amazing device your brain can be if you give it time to work the way it was designed to!

I recently heard about a Chinese student who wanted a visa to come to America. He was told, "No more are being issued, come back next year."

He said, "No problem. Thank you for the opportunity. Would morning or afternoon be better?"

Here's how we took what some people would call a "problem" and turned it into an wonderful opportunity.

Barry

It was March of 1978. After just three years in business (and a few very successful products), we were going down the tubes! Going bankrupt! With the cash flow the way it was, it would only be a few months until we would be closing the doors. But how did this happen? We were the hotshots! The kids who'd made good! Articles had been written about us calling us "the kings of television mail order," and yet we weren't going to make it through our third year. We just had to do something to survive. We had started to sell the Miracle Painter retail in drugstore chains. We must have been taking the drugs they were selling when we made that decision because any profits we thought we were going to make were just hallucinations. Getting payment from the drug chains was almost impossible and it was about to put us out of business.

The retailing of the Miracle Painter combined with our failure to come up with another real winning television product for almost two years was one of the reasons we found ourselves in desperate straits. Boy, did we ever have a problem, or so we thought. What we had was an opportunity! We just didn't know it yet.

Going to work in the morning was no longer a fun thing. It seemed that every time the phone rang it was another vendor screaming for payment. Our bank balance was so low that the bank took back the free toaster it gave us when we opened the account. Our only way out was to come up with another miracle product, but we were fresh out of miracles. Even if we came up with a fabulous product, it was obvious that the multitude of TV stations would not let us air the commercials because we were behind in payments. It seemed as if we were trapped in a corner and there was no way out.

Every day started with a "State of the Business" meeting. In the good old days (the previous year) we would talk about how much money we were making, how brilliant we were, and we'd pat each other on the back. Now it seemed that all our discussions revolved around how little money we were taking in, how much money we owed to how many people, and when our cash would run out.

Nevertheless, we plunged forward, exploring ideas and possible future products.

We had been in contact with Mirro Aluminum, at that time the largest cookware manufacturer in the United States, and had begun discussions with them exploring the possibility of marketing a line of pots and pans. The biggest problem we had was that Mirro needed at

75

least six months to produce the set of cookware necessary to meet our price points. We would be broke long before then. Mickey was having ongoing discussions with a small 50-year-old company named Quikut in Fremont, Ohio, that manufactured kitchen knives that they sold in supermarket bins. They told us that if we chose any knives that were in their catalog, they would be able to produce them instantly. Although their ability to produce was music to our ears, the idea of selling kitchen knives to households that already owned them did not excite us. In the past, everything we had sold successfully was either unique or we had an exclusive.

Because Quikut's knives had nothing really unique about them, it would be almost impossible to sell them on TV, even if they gave us an exclusive. However, we asked them for samples of all their knives just to see if we could come up with any ideas. We also did some research and found that there were already knives being sold via TV.

One offer was a set of English Sheffield knives being sold for $7.99 and the other was a carving knife from Quikut that was selling for $3.99. It took some prodding, but we found out that neither offer was doing well. So we dropped the idea and started looking elsewhere for our next miracle.

It seemed that everything else we thought of ran into the same problem that Mirro had: It would take at least six months to get production going.

The clock was steadily ticking toward our demise. Eventually it became obvious to us that the only way out of this predicament was to try and sell some type of knife offer on TV. It really didn't matter if the product was a big winner. We just needed to get some cash flow going. It seemed that selling knives was the only way to stay in business. We had already paid a production facility in Boston, so our credit was good with them. If we could somehow come up with an idea on how to market the knives, we would at least have a place to produce the commercial.

First up on the list was to look at and play with every knife that Quikut manufactured. As it turned out, they produced more than 70 different items ranging from a carving knife to various food decorating and garnishing tools. The next problem was to try and pick out everything that we thought should go into the offer.

No Problemos

Naturally we wanted a carving knife, and Quikut had one with a normally serrated edge on the bottom and a heavily serrated edge on the top that could be used to cut frozen food. We all felt strongly that the double-edged carving knife should be part of the offer, but what else should we add? We needed to be very cost-conscious because we felt the retail price could be no more than $9.95. That meant that if we had any hope of being profitable, we could spend no more than $3 for all the pieces that would make up our offer. The carving knife would cost us 75 cents, so we were 25 percent there and we only had one piece. Mickey felt very strongly that the more pieces we offered, the better chance we had for a successful product. We all agreed but, as usual, I was the anchor carefully monitoring every penny.

Ed felt that we should definitely add the carving fork, but I wasn't sure because of its cost. Another 75 cents. We would be at 50 percent of our possible expenditure with only two pieces. It sure wasn't looking good.

Ed ventured, "It sure would be great to have 10 pieces for $10. Then it would seem to the customers that they were getting every knife for no more than a dollar a piece."

Mickey said, "Not only that, but if we surround the knives with food, it would make the offer seem like they were getting not only the knives, but the food as well. It would look voluminous!"

Little did I realize that his formula was to lead us in a new direction for years to come. Surrounding our kitchen product offers with lots of food is something we dubbed "beauty shots."

After spending the rest of the day examining the various products in the line, we adjourned until morning. When we arrived the next morning we summoned our creative director and quickly locked the outer doors that connected the rest of the building to our wing. No one was going to disturb our meeting. We unplugged the phones and went about trying to select the rest of the knives that would be included in the offer.

Looking at the cost sheet it became obvious to all of us that because steak knives were only 19 cents each, many should be included in the offer. Let's face it: no one ever has enough steak knives.

The Wisdom of Ginsu

"Let's see, how many can we afford?" I asked. "If we add six steak knives, we'll be at $2.64. That leaves very little room for anything else."

But was that enough to get the American public to spend $10? None of us thought so. We also felt that with these eight pieces, we wouldn't have enough magic in the commercial.

What else could we add to make it better? That's where our British partner's pitchman experience really helped. In the past, in England, they had pitched food garnishing tools on street corners and at flea markets. In Quikut's inventory there was a food decorating tool called a spiral slicer. With my limited kitchen experience (about all I had ever done in the kitchen was burn toast), I had no idea what this strange-looking device actually did.

Mickey of course did know, and explained, "It goes into the top of a potato and spirals around and around until it makes a great potato garnish."

I kept my mouth shut because I had no idea what a potato garnish was and because we could buy this thing for only 11 cents and Mickey assured us it would be magical on TV.

Two weeks went by and finally we all agreed on the 10 pieces that would be included in the set. However, none of us felt that we had a winner. Every household in the United States had nothing if it didn't have knives. No matter how good we made the knives look, we felt that not enough people would buy them to make the effort profitable. We had to come up with some kind of crazy idea to market them.

We started working on our layout for the commercial.

Ed said, "We should feature the carving knife."

There were many other opinions but, as always, my vote went with Ed. There were two reasons:

1. I felt he was right.
2. We had agreed to never disagree with each other in front of others. Because we were not only partners but also best friends, we felt that it was important to always show unity in front of others. When we were alone the gloves could come off.

No Problemos

After two days of discussion it was finally agreed that the first knife shown would be the double-edged carver. We then discussed what the knife should be doing. At this time we had absolutely no idea how sharp these babies were.

"How about hacking wood and cutting paper?"

Would it work?

"What about cutting a rubber hose and then a tomato?"

"How about showing the double-edged knife cutting a frozen chicken?"

"Would it cut through a tire?"

The discussion seemed as if it would never end. We did agree on one thing that became one of our trademark classics. We would cut something ridiculous such as a tire to show how strong and sharp the knife was. Then we would immediately cut food such as a slice of bread to show that it remained sharp.

We could say, "It can cut a nail and still slice a tomato paper thin." On camera we would do this seamlessly, without an edit. This would prove to the viewer that there were no camera tricks involved and that the knives actually worked.

We ordered frozen chickens, rubber hoses, tomatoes, soda cans, and all sorts of other items and did our test research in Ed's office. At day's end, Ed suggested that we all go home and start cutting up all the frozen stuff we had. One thing was apparent the next morning. Everyone was amazed at how these knives cut all of the items we selected. Not only food, but the crazy stuff as well—soda cans, nails, tires hoses, you name it. We wondered if we could translate that magic to the small screen.

Mickey mentioned that he knew a geezer (rhyming slang for *guy*) in Canada who was an expert with kitchen knives at flea markets. Phil felt that we should use this fellow to do the demonstration in the commercial, as he had been doing magic with knives for years. We agreed.

Now that we had an idea of what the commercial would look like, we needed a name for the knife set and a marketing method. Little did we realize that we would have to spend more than 12 days working together before we would come up with the final concept and more than 600 man-hours just writing the opening 10 seconds.

No matter what idea someone came up with or what name he liked, someone else invariably hated it.

After days of discussion, Ed felt that American quality wasn't quite good enough for this offer even though the products were American-made. He felt that we had to add mystery to the product.

He said, "What if we gave the illusion that it was an imported product? What if we pretended it was made somewhere overseas?"

My eyes lit up at this suggestion because not only did I think it was a great idea, but I wanted to do anything that would get this thing on TV ASAP.

"Go on, Ed," I said. "How would you go about it?"

"I'll give you an example," said Ed. "What if we used an announcer with an English accent and we clanged two carving knives together like they do in the Wilkinson razor blade commercials. But, of course, we would never say that they were made in England. Everyone would just assume that they were made in England and of Wilkinson quality."

I thought Ed's idea was great. It was just what we needed. The product desperately needed an identity and Ed had found a way to give it one, but I insisted that we continue to explore the idea, and we did...for three days. We were close to making it the final concept when I realized what had been bothering me. This whole offer revolved around hitting two carving knives together like the swords Wilkinson banged together in its commercial. Without this graphic image, it just wouldn't work. The problem was that if we used that image, the consumer would expect to receive two carving knives. When we sold the Miracle Painter we showed a man painting a ceiling with the Miracle Painter attached to a broomstick. We actually received complaints from people because they didn't receive a broomstick. The complaints would never end if we opened the spot that way. We would have to include two carving knives, I argued. That would put our costs over the top and make the product unprofitable.

No Problemos

The other thing at the back of my mind was that the competing English Sheffield knife offer had failed, and that was a genuine English product very similar to our offer.

"Maybe Americans just don't want English knives," I offered.

That statement gave everyone pause. Even Ed had to agree that if we went in the English direction, we were asking for trouble.

Phil suggested we try another country.

Even though no one was too happy with me for bursting the bubble, they agreed.

The next discussion involved Germany and the Germans' ability to produce exacting, fine, and strong products. We discussed Leica cameras, Hasselblads, Mercedes-Benz, and then decided on German steel. We could build the commercial on the idea that German steel was the best. After two days of discussions we knew we had a few problems. One was a legal problem. We would definitely be implying that the steel in our blades was from Germany, and fraud was not something we were interested in. Another problem was finding a good opening for the spot and a good name for the product. We had spent a long time on this and had come up with nothing promising. German is a very hard-sounding language, and no matter what we came up with, it didn't sound good.

We spent the next few days mentally exploring Russia and the Scandinavian countries, but all to no avail. It seemed that none of these countries had ever manufactured anything original or eye-catching.

France was famous for its wine, but we couldn't find a tie-in. We explored the idea of a French chef introducing the product, but we just couldn't get enthused about the idea.

Next came the Arab countries. There were a lot of possibilities in Arabia. We though of a Sinbad or a Lawrence of Arabia–type of character doing the demonstration of the knives. But nothing we tried worked.

We were all exhausted, depressed, and burnt out. We had nowhere to go but the Far East.

So, we mentally traveled to Japan. Japan was full of useful concepts. We thought of naming the product "The Hari-Kari Set," but we quickly changed our minds when we realized that someone might take it literally and commit hari-kari. (Our attorneys loved that one, thinking about all the legal defense work they would get.) Next, the product came close to being named "The Samurai Set," but in considering how to open a commercial for the Samurai we had difficulty.

Finally, we decided that a great opening for the commercial (which was two minutes long) would be to compare our knife to a karate chop. So, we came up with the idea of using a karate chop on a wooden board and then on a tomato while saying, "In Japan the hand can be used as a knife, but that method doesn't work on a tomato." We felt that the shock value of seeing a tomato squashed by a karate chop would surprise and entertain viewers and keep them interested in seeing the rest of the commercial.

Boy, were we right!

Now that we had the opening, what could we do in the body of the spot? We each took the knives home and started cutting everything in sight! Would it cut a tree branch? Sure! We opened the hood on our cars and started to cut the radiator hose to see if it would cut that! Sure did! A call to AAA solved that zealous experiment. Now, would it cut a tire? We got really brilliant and decided to cut the spare tire rather than the one on the car. It worked like a charm. Next were nails, linoleum, and even a tin can.

Now, how could we present this to our future customers? Because we had so many knives and because we wanted to create tremendous value, we decided to pause after each item in the set and say, "But Wait! There's More!" This line has now been used by everyone from Burger King to Southwest Airlines!

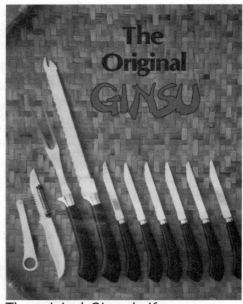

The original Ginsu knife.

82

No Problemos

After all this, what were we going to call the product? Would it be Samurai?

Well, in a session after 600 hours of creative development, with our eyes bleary, we became silly and started talking pseudo-Japanese. One of us uttered the word *Ginsu*, and a legend was born!

But wait! There's more!

Okay, we now had a product that tested fabulously. In our tests on various stations that would still do business with us, the Ginsu appeared to be our best product ever. Our advertising cost to get an order was coming in at around $1; deducting the cost of the product and overhead expenses, we would be left with a profit of approximately $4. If we could crank sales up to 20,000 units a week, we could be out of debt in a no time at all.

However, we were in a classic "catch-22" situation. Most of the TV stations had shut the door on us. We needed to air the commercials on all the stations, but most of them wouldn't consider letting us on the air without cash up front. We desperately needed all our cash flow for payroll and overhead, and there was no money left over for the stations. We had taken ourselves off the payroll a long time before in order to keep the business afloat. Even worse, the way our business worked when we launched a new product was that 90 percent of our orders would be CODs and only 10 percent were prepaid by checks. So for us to get paid for 90 percent of our orders we had to first ship the product via UPS COD and wait three or four weeks to receive the money. We were on enough stations to produce about 5,000 Ginsu orders a week, but that meant we would only get 500 prepaid orders a week and, at $10 apiece, only $5,000 would be coming in from our new product. We were fortunate on two counts:

1. We managed to stay fairly current with UPS, as they were our lifeblood.

2. The manufacturer of the knives had no idea about our financial situation and would be only too happy to drop ship the product from its factory direct to our customers and grant us 30 days' credit.

It seemed as if we had reached another dead end.

In meeting after meeting we discussed the issue, and of course everyone's eyes looked to Ed and myself as the deep pockets. Surely, we would dig deeper and come up with some advertising dollars. Ed and I had already put up a ton of money just to keep the company going, and we weren't crazy about going any deeper.

In one of our meetings I decided to look at the situation a little differently. Because our advertising cost per order was $1, it meant that if we spent $1,000 on advertising, we would get 1,000 orders, and 10 percent of those orders (100) would be prepaid by check. That meant that a $1,000 TV expenditure was sure to bring 100 checks for $10. Those prepaid orders would cover the cost of advertising. Because all prepaid check orders went directly to the TV stations, what if we could get the stations to keep those orders as payment for their advertising? In that case, we wouldn't have to lay out any additional cash, we could keep the cash flow we currently had, which was enough to keep the doors open, and we would be able to expand the program. I told our controller, who was fighting a losing battle with the stations to try the plan with a few people he had a good relationship with. I told him to say, "Not only will this plan ensure that you get paid for current advertising, but it will get your old balances paid off quickly." He made a few calls, and this plan was accepted. Furthermore, the stations didn't want to endorse the checks, so they decided to forward them to us for deposit and gave us seven days to send them the money. If a station objected to the plan, the reps were told about all the other stations that had gone along with the plan and that we had an obligation to pay off old balances first to the people who were working with us. Eventually, everyone went our way. We quickly generated enough cash to pay everyone off and continue the program.

Opportunity met; problem solved! In other words, no problemos!

Little did we know at the time that we had just "given birth" to a brand name that would become legendary with amazing recall percentages among consumers, and even different generations, more than three decades after it last aired on television! Remember that the commercials we created were not designed to generate "top of mind" brand awareness. This was "act now" marketing: leave your TV, call an 800 number, give your credit card information to a stranger, then wait six weeks to get the product. Our offers were structured to create that "act now" emotional response and desire, which it clearly did, as evidenced by more than $40 million in sales. And yet, almost 30 years later, if you ask the average person to name a sharp knife, almost all of them will say Ginsu.

On a funny note, I remember one day one of our employees came running in looking extremely frightened and out of breath. He told us that he had run down to our office because the Japanese embassy had just called and said the word *Ginsu* was a "nasty sexual slang term having to do with mothers." I can't repeat it here. Anyway, we panicked. Millions of dollars in advertising was at stake, as well as our future. Barry and I were just about to commit hari-kari when the employee laughed and said he was just kidding, it was just a joke.

We were all relieved when he told us, and I smiled. Then I put my arm around the guy's shoulder and said, "You're a real no-good Ginsu. Not only that, but you're Ginsu fired, you little Ginsu. You almost gave us a Ginsu heart attack. I don't want to ever see your Ginsu face around here again." I waited for him to panic and then told him I, too, was "only joking." Little did we know at the time that the literal translation of "Ginsu" was: "You won't have to work another day in your life."

These particular problem situations turned out to be the biggest opportunity of our lives. Not only did we save the company, but we created a marketing legend and ensured our financial futures!

Problem or opportunity? It all depends on how you look at things. No matter what the next challenge looks like, sounds like, or seems like, if your approach is "no problemos," it's just another puzzle for you to solve, not a crisis for you to overcome.

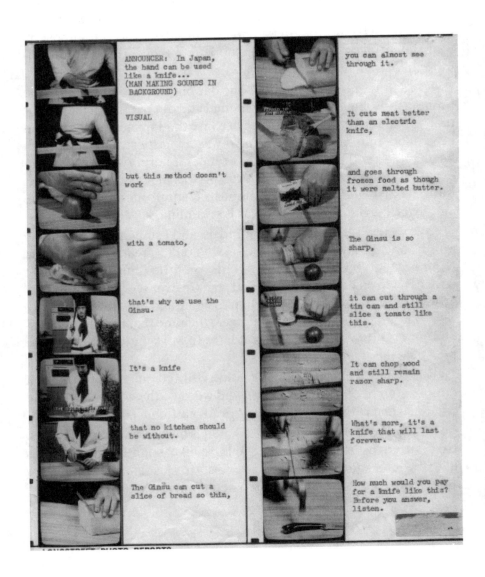

ANNOUNCER: In Japan, the hand can be used like a knife... (MAN MAKING SOUNDS IN BACKGROUND)

VISUAL

but this method doesn't work

with a tomato,

that's why we use the Ginsu.

It's a knife

that no kitchen should be without.

The Ginsu can cut a slice of bread so thin,

you can almost see through it.

It cuts meat better than an electric knife,

and goes through frozen food as though it were melted butter.

The Ginsu is so sharp,

it can cut through a tin can and still slice a tomato like this.

It can chop wood and still remain razor sharp.

What's more, it's a knife that will last forever.

How much would you pay for a knife like this? Before you answer, listen.

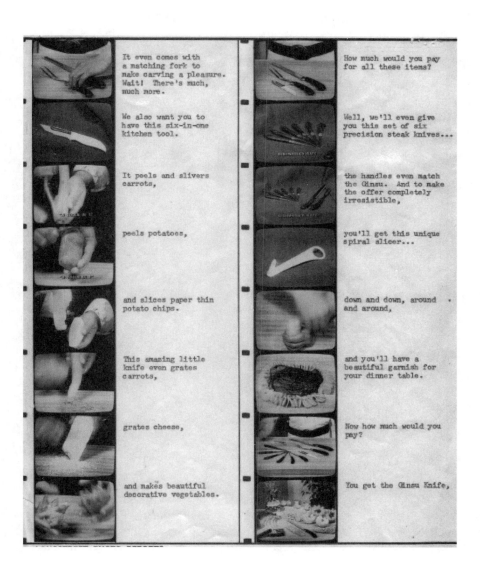

It even comes with
a matching fork to
make carving a pleasure.
Wait! There's much,
much more.

We also want you to
have this six-in-one
kitchen tool.

It peels and slivers
carrots,

peels potatoes,

and slices paper thin
potato chips.

This amazing little
knife even grates
carrots,

grates cheese,

and makes beautiful
decorative vegetables.

How much would you pay
for all these items?

Well, we'll even give
you this set of six
precision steak knives...

the handles even match
the Ginsu. And to make
the offer completely
irresistible,

you'll get this unique
spiral slicer...

down and down, around
and around,

and you'll have a
beautiful garnish for
your dinner table.

Now how much would you
pay?

You get the Ginsu Knife,

87

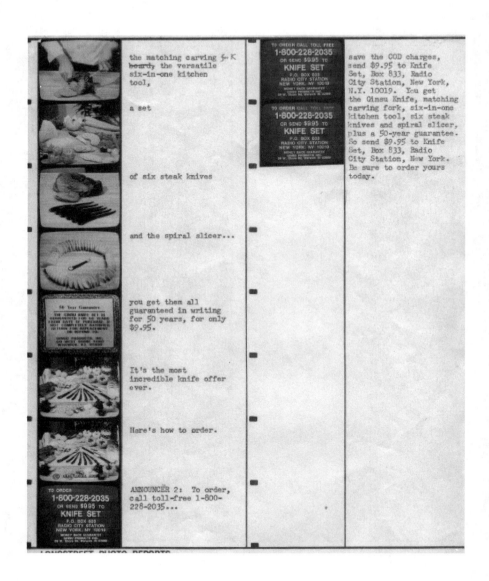

the matching carving fork, boardy the versatile six-in-one kitchen tool,

a set

of six steak knives

and the spiral slicer...

you get them all guaranteed in writing for 50 years, for only $9.95.

It's the most incredible knife offer ever.

Here's how to order.

ANNOUNCER 2: To order, call toll-free 1-800-228-2035...

TO ORDER CALL TOLL FREE
1-800-228-2035
OR SEND $9.95 TO
KNIFE SET
P.O. BOX 833
RADIO CITY STATION
NEW YORK, NY 10019

TO ORDER CALL TOLL FREE
1-800-228-2035
OR SEND $9.95 TO
KNIFE SET
P.O. BOX 833
RADIO CITY STATION
NEW YORK, NY 10019

save the COD charges, send $9.95 to Knife Set, Box 833, Radio City Station, New York, N.Y. 10019. You get the Ginsu Knife, matching carving fork, six-in-one kitchen tool, six steak knives and spiral slicer, plus a 50-year guarantee. So send $9.95 to Knife Set, Box 833, Radio City Station, New York. Be sure to order yours today.

9

Get Back to Them,
or They'll Get
Someone Else

Barry

Want a great way to increase business, get promoted, be successful, and have everyone say how great you are? Drumroll please…. Return your phone calls! Think about it for a minute: don't you just hate it when people don't return your calls? It works both ways. Most people get very agitated, if not offended, when you don't return their calls. It's crazy, but we now accept that it will take two or three calls before we get one in return, and we can't stop talking about how nice someone is when he or she returns our first call. How many people reading this book have started a telephone conversation with someone who calls back quickly, saying, appreciatively, "Thanks for calling me back"? When you think about it, why

89

should we be thanking someone for performing the most basic of business courtesies? I wonder what our life would have been like if we didn't return the call from the (Quikut) Ginsu factory? Perhaps someone else would be writing this book.

Don't return your calls and you'll never know if you missed that big deal or opportunity that could have changed your life. That important call could be right there on hold, and you are blowing it off by telling your receptionist or secretary, "Put them in voice mail." If you are that good to be able to know which calls are important and which ones are not, then you should be in Las Vegas instead of reading this book on how to improve your life. For every phone call you return promptly, you create an ambassador of goodwill…for you! For every call you blow off, who knows?

Now perhaps you are one of those people who doesn't return phone calls because you have nothing to say. Nothing has changed since the last time you spoke and you still have no answer to give the person who is calling. No decision has been made yet, so why call back or take the call? Good strategy, right? Wrong. Why? Because it's unprofessional and could come back to bite you in the butt someday. What could be easier and have more of an effect in creating an advocate for you than saying, "I still don't have an answer, but check back with me in a couple of weeks" (in the case of a vendor) or "I'll get back to you as soon as I have the answer" (in the case of a client). That 30-second call leaves the caller with the lasting impression that you are a thoughtful, courteous, and efficient person to take the time and make the effort to update him. How do you know what role that person will have on your life in the future? You don't. Perhaps he will someday be in a position to give you or your son or daughter a job. Or maybe you'll need a favor someday. Treat all these people as if they will be back in your life someday and will help you. You will be amazed at how fast the word will travel about you and how much your career or business will benefit from this small change, even though you may never hear directly what other people are saying about you in a positive way.

With regard to customer service, have you noticed how much things have deteriorated? It seems that no one cares about business anymore. People are generally rude and lazy, and try to make you think they are doing you a favor just taking your money. Is that the sound of opportunity knocking? You bet it is, so answer the door! Just do the opposite. Be polite, work hard, and treat people right and you'll be amazed at how quickly your career or business is "fast tracked."

We have become so accustomed to bad service that it now shrouds itself as routine. We just don't expect anything more. Is it any wonder that when someone goes above and beyond the call of duty, we just cannot stop talking about him? Has he gone above and beyond? No! Years ago, that was the level of service everyone expected, and got. In the movie *Back to the Future*, remember the scene when a car drives up to the Texaco station and four men come out in uniforms to fill the tank, wash the windshield, check the air in the tires, and more? Now *that* was service!

We have been in a downward slope ever since. Here are a few examples of service and people that Ed and I have dubbed "What the *hell* were you thinking?"

Ed

In the ad business, some salespeople show up late for appointments and don't apologize. They leave money on the table by not understanding the art of negotiation or simply not caring.

I've said to many salespeople, "I'm sorry. I can't give you any money on this media buy."

Many have responded with, "Oh, okay, perhaps next time."

I can't tell you how many times I just wanted to grab them firmly but gently by the shoulders and say, "Ask me why you didn't get the order, please just ask me why. I want to negotiate. Talk to me. Don't you want to make this sale?"

I remember recently going to my favorite hotel in Disney World. When the taxi pulled up, no one was around to take my bags. I carried my own bags in and asked the person at the registration desk where all the wonderful young and polite bellman had gone.

He replied, "All of the great bellman were promoted to managers and now we can't find anyone to replace them. We have little to pick from now."

The Wisdom of Ginsu

No wonder even just "good" customer service stands out so much in the 21st century.

Back to the ad business. Very often, the people who work at these various stations and networks don't even return their phone calls. Sometimes when we are looking to spend money we can't even find the sales rep. It might take two or three calls from us for her to call us back. I was trying to reach a representative once on an urgent matter regarding a radio schedule I had booked with her. Because she was out of the office, in desperation I called her cell phone all day to no avail. When she finally returned my call the next day, I said, "Where have you been? I called your cell phone all day yesterday."

She said, "Oh, I never answer my cell phone."

Oh. I see. What a unique and senseless way to waste money and, at the same time, prevent people from giving you more money.

Unfortunately, this is a true story. Now, I don't want to give the ad business a black eye, because the majority of the sales representatives I know are hardworking and conscientious. But a few of them, as I like to say, "Don't get it!" Perhaps they should double click the refresh icon on the way they think!

People ask me all the time, "Why is your business so successful when many in your industry are failing?" Simple, I do the basics: return phone calls. Always work in the best interest of my clients. Make my clients and customers feel special. I under-promise and over-deliver. I tell them how much I appreciate their business, and mean it. It's like the cartoon I once read. A salesman goes into a client's office with a big sign that says, "We want your business and we'll kiss your ass to get it." Now, that's the way to get business!

Thanks to the people who don't get it yet! Just think, if they didn't exist, it would be even more difficult to make money than it already is.

Not returning phone calls is as silly as what some companies do unwittingly to torture their consumers. They use a voice-mail receptionist that leads to voice mail for departments that leads to voice mail for individuals. Even the voice mail has voice mail!

"Hi, Ima Unareachable's voice mail is full, if you'd like to leave a message, you can do so in our company's general mailbox."

Ever try to reach a living person at one of these companies?

How about retail stores? Same thing. Why don't they just say, "Hi, we don't have anyone who can talk to you right now, so if you drive all the way down to our store, we'll be happy to tell you we don't have that in stock."

What's next, will bad customer service be available in all languages?

"Hi, if you would like bad service in English, press 1; bad service in Spanish, press 2."

What these companies seem to be saying is, "We'd rather find a new customer than hang on to an old one." Which is really no different than saying, "I'd rather buy a new engine than change the oil in this one!"

Take my most recent encounter with a famous-name super hardware store. I wanted to buy a fence for my yard. I made an appointment for the installer to come over one day between 8 a.m. and 8 p.m. No show. I called to complain, and after 20 minutes of voice-mail hell, I was promised a return phone call with a reason why the installer was a no-show. Nothing. Called again, nothing. Called again, nothing. They made me feel like I was Yasser Arafat waiting for Ariel Sharon to invite me over for dinner!

They didn't get back to me, so I got someone else. Not only did their competitor show up on time, but they sold me a fence and now have all of my business.

Now I don't want to pick on these giant hardware superstores, because I'm sure the majority of their workers are hardworking and conscientious, but what is going on here? Where has all the customer service gone? Is there some new subliminal mantra being played in the store's music system that is saying, "Screw the customer; we'll get new ones"? Makes you wonder.

Hey, why should I have to work that hard to give my money away? Never forget this if you are in a client/service business. Your job is to give service, not receive it.

Do you have any calls you haven't returned over the last several months? Call them all today and apologize for not calling sooner. Don't prioritize them, don't rule any out, and don't make any judgments. If you don't finish them all today, cross off the ones you make and finish the rest tomorrow. Or e-mail them some response to "keep the ball rolling."

"But I don't have the time!" you say.

Are you kidding? How can you be too busy to take advantage of a call that could literally change your life? How do you know which one it is? You don't. What you can be sure of is that if you don't return your phone calls, you are decreasing the odds of good things happening to and for you. And can you really afford to lessen your chances for success, when other people are increasing theirs?

Nothing you ever do in business is easier to do and has a better chance for success than returning phone calls—promptly. It's a great way to increase business.

So, is it any wonder that returning phone calls (and e-mails) is both the easiest way to keep your clients happy and discover new ones? And if you're in the client-service business and don't return phone calls, you're dead.

Who would be dumb enough to do that? Many companies whose bread and butter is customer service do it constantly. Do it right and you'll set yourself apart from competitors and other people as being organized, smart, responsive, helpful, kind, and caring simply because the majority of us are "too busy" for what used to be simple, automatic courtesy.

So, here's the deal and the rule we live by. Do what everybody is not doing. Provide really good customer service in a time when it's rare (and everybody is begging for it) and you will be a leader in your industry.

Think something as simple as not returning a phone call can't be expensive. Listen to this:

When we first wanted to do a possible nonstick cookware offer, we naturally contacted as many pots and pans manufacturers as we could find. Mirro Aluminum, the largest manufacturer of cookware in the United States at the time, got back to us quickly and suggested that it send a company representative to meet with us and discuss our needs. Mirro Aluminum followed up right away, and within days we were having serious discussions. Believe it or not, some of the other companies didn't even return our calls. They were too busy trying to sell their products to K-Mart and other outlets, or didn't take us seriously. What did it cost them because they didn't get back to us? Well, let's see, we sold about three million sets of cookware for about $80 million. We paid somewhere in the vicinity of $30 to $35 million for all of our cookware sets.

Remember, it's up to you to be responsive and follow up with folks who are trying to give you money, and you never know which phone call that's going to be. If someone calls you, whether you know who it is or what he wants or not, "get back to them, or they'll get someone else."

When in Doubt, Blow It Out

Barry

Don't stay married to ideas that you love, that don't work. Start over—you can do better. Many a career or project have been sunk by getting emotional over an idea. Also, when writing, whether it be a business report, TV commercial, or school paper, remember, there's no such thing as good writing, only good rewriting. How many times have you tried to write something about an idea you had? You start with the idea topic and then you freeze. Nothing happens. You just cannot develop the idea or thought. Blow it out! Get rid of it and start over. If it's not coming, don't force it. It will only show up as forced work. Start over. You'll get better results and save yourself a hell of a lot of time! And if you write for others, remember, work hard, and you'll be *reworded* (that's not a misprint; it's *reworded* not *rewarded*!).

Ed

How many of us have bought stock in companies whose only product was their price? We never knew what they did, or where they were located, or ever bothered to do any research whatsoever! We just bought it because someone said, "It's going to the moon." That alone is bad, but when the stock price started to go down, we may have had some doubts, but we never blew it out. We held, hoping it would recover. It never did. And every time it fell a few more points, we bought more to average down our costs. That's like trying to catch a falling knife. We end up holding a stock that may be 60 to 70 percent less than we paid. A 20-ercent stop loss would have blown the stock out and limited our losses. I remember reading a great line about investing. Someone asked a very successful investor what his strategy was for making millions in the market. He said, "I always sold too soon." In other words, he always blew them out!

Human nature is against us on this one. It seems that most of us are not willing to blow things out when we should. It's hard for us to accept that we were wrong because of ego. Hard for us to sell something for less than we paid. Hard to admit we made a mistake. This kind of thinking is very expensive. Over the last 20 years I've seen hundreds of people who truly believe they have the next Ginsu. A few did, but most didn't. What's incredible is I can always tell when these people have an emotional involvement with their products and ideas. How? They come to me for advice, and when they get it, they refuse to believe it. They sit in my office and come up with so many excuses why I might be wrong; leave and spend thousands of dollars trying to prove me wrong. I think you can figure out how this scenario ends. The same goes for a house you put on the market. In the northeast, where I live, I remember a woman not accepting an offer I made on her house in early August because I was a few thousand dollars off the asking price. She had already moved and was paying two mortgages. She was so emotionally attached to the house that she was insulted by my offer. As you may know, it gets pretty cold around here, so instead of blowing the house out, she sat on it all winter and paid more than the difference in the price I offered by heating it all winter, and paying the mortgage, taxes, and other expenses. When she came to her senses, and wanted to accept my offer, the market conditions had changed and the house was worthless.

It's the same for cars or anything that we become emotionally involved with. Remember that the emotion is all yours, not anyone else's. I apply this rule to almost everything in life. Did you ever hear Dr. Laura on the radio? I wish I had a dollar for every woman who calls and talks about an abusive marriage. They say, "He did this or that to me because I got him mad," or "He hits me but he really loves me." Get real! Dr. Laura always gets angry and tells the listener to leave, in other words, "blow him out." He's not working, and neither is your relationship! Good advice.

Here's how we put this concept to work for us:

In late 1980, we marketed a second Ginsu knife set with completely different knives. We called it Ginsu II. We felt we needed to have all new knives so we could attract a new audience for the product, as well as appeal to the previous buyers of the first Ginsu knife set. We decided to fly out to the factory in Freemont, Ohio. Well, Freemont is one of those places that you can't get to easily. You can fly to Cleveland and then drive forever, or you can fly to Detroit and drive around one of those great lakes. Because we didn't want it to be an overnight trip, we opted to fly to Detroit and hired a small, twin-engine aircraft to fly us over the lake

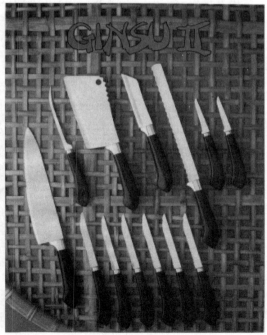

Ginsu II.

to Freemont. Upon arrival we sat in the conference room and spent hours going over every product that the manufacturer Quikut sold. Then we returned to Rhode Island via the same route and had samples of all the knives sent to us. After countless hours hacking tomatoes, trees, watermelons, and even linoleum, we started to finalize the product selection. The problem we faced was that we had no one knife that could be a star attraction like we had in the original Ginsu offer. So we invented one and we patented it. Never before had there been a carving knife that had a straight and a serrated edge on the same blade. This ingenious knife would be our star. We also had decided to use a utility knife, an assortment of garnishing tools, and even a cleaver in the offer. Something else was needed, and we decided to go back to the factory once again to finalize product selection and pricing. To accomplish the trip in a single day and accommodate additional staff that we brought along, we chartered a private jet after we learned that there was a small airport a few miles from the factory. The meeting went successfully and, after we showed them our new knife invention, the Quikut people assured us that it wouldn't be a problem to make the new knife. We finally settled on the following for the offer:

1. Our new patented knife.
2. Bread-slicing knife.

Ginsu II beauty shot.

3. Cleaver with meat tenderizer.
4. Utility knife.
5. Garnishing tool.
6. Paring knife.
7. Second paring knife.
8. Fruit and vegetable knife.

Barry

We had opened the first commercial with Ed karate chopping a tomato. For this second set of knives we needed to do something different. After many creative meetings we decided that Ed should go flying through the air and end up karate kicking a watermelon. We could use the newly invented knife to slice a melon in half and show that it was not only better than a foot for slicing watermelons, but it was

Ed karate kicking board in Ginsu II.

also better than other knives. It was December and there wasn't a watermelon to be seen anywhere in the northeast. We managed to locate some in Florida and we had a dozen watermelons flown up to Rhode Island, where we were filming the commercial. We thought we would need quite a few takes and melons before the shot would be good enough to use in the opening scene. Of course, because we had all those melons in stock, Ed went flying through the air and his foot landed perfectly, right in the center of the watermelon and practically tore it apart. It was first-take perfection! We didn't need the extra melons, so we gave them to our staff and crew and we all enjoyed watermelon for the holidays.

The Wisdom of Ginsu

We charged $19.95 for the second Ginsu knife set, which consisted of seven different knives and a set of food-garnishing tools. But something was wrong because the CPO (advertising cost per order) was too high and we were losing close to $2 on every order.

We needed to generate more business—and fast.

Ed

By now, Ginsu was a household name and a million people had already bought the product. We knew they liked it. So what was wrong? Either we weren't offering the consumers enough value or we had sold so many of the first Ginsu set that people didn't want the second one.

Golden one million Ginsus.

We went back to the drawing board. We thought, "What if we added six steak knives the way we did with the first set? Did every home already have enough steak knives? Can anyone ever have enough steak knives?" We decided to throw in six steak knives and blow out the food garnishing tools. The garnishing tools were the perfect candidates to be blown out because they cost as much as six steak knives.

When in Doubt, Blow It Out

As far as we were concerned, when you're selling knives, garnishing tools are expendable. We found some old footage we had shot of six steak knives and edited it into the commercial in place of the garnishing footage. So now, instead of seven knives in the package, we were offering a total of 13. We were pretty sure that this would make the offer a lot more appealing—and it did.

The response was amazing. With Ginsu I, we sold about a million sets. With Ginsu II, we sold even more.

Now, how did we know that six more steak knives would make all the difference?

We didn't know. We trusted our gut instincts, which turned out to be right. We took what we had and blew it out. We replaced it with the six steak knives. The rest is history.

Nowadays, companies selling knives on television might make that decision very differently. They'd pay a lot of money for researchers to sit behind a one-way mirror as a group of consumers talked about the product. They'd convene focus groups representing various ages and ethnicities who would talk a little more. Weeks later, after more meetings, more evaluations, and more money spent, they would probably conclude that what the offer really needed was six steak knives; the exact same conclusion you reached on your own, only now it has cost you a lot more time and money. Sometimes your gut is a better indicator of success than scientific "evidence." How do you know when? You don't. That's why they call it "gut instinct."

How did we know what to blow out? You know that little voice inside your head that dares you to do things that you are afraid to do? Listen to it. It's not the voice of insanity, it's the voice of reason. It's gut instinct! It's the same voice that tells you the difference between right and wrong. If you ignore it, it will cost you. Learn to listen to your adventurous, entrepreneurial, risk-taking natural spirit. It's there for a reason and, without it, nothing great will ever be accomplished.

So many people in business are afraid to trust their gut instincts. Often, gut instinct is nothing more than good common sense, the result of years of close observation and personal experience.

Look at it as if it were a hard drive on your computer. Over the years, you add various programs and information that comes with experience. Then, without even knowing what's there, you find yourself drawing on it. After every success in your life, you can afford to trust your gut a little more. The lesson? You know a lot more than you think you do!

So remember these six words when something is just "not happening," when something you thought was right is clearly wrong, when you're just not sure which way to turn, or when you just have no idea at all what to do: "When in doubt, blow it out!"

Barry hammering Ginsu knife handle.

Ed slicing carrots with Ginsu knife.

Ed at work.

Barry at work.

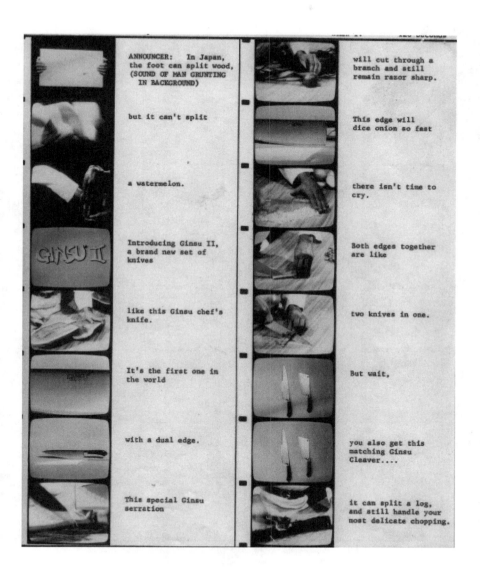

ANNOUNCER: In Japan, the foot can split wood, (SOUND OF MAN GRUNTING IN BACKGROUND)

but it can't split

a watermelon.

Introducing Ginsu II, a brand new set of knives

like this Ginsu chef's knife.

It's the first one in the world

with a dual edge.

This special Ginsu serration

will cut through a branch and still remain razor sharp.

This edge will dice onion so fast

there isn't time to cry.

Both edges together are like

two knives in one.

But wait,

you also get this matching Ginsu Cleaver....

it can split a log, and still handle your most delicate chopping.

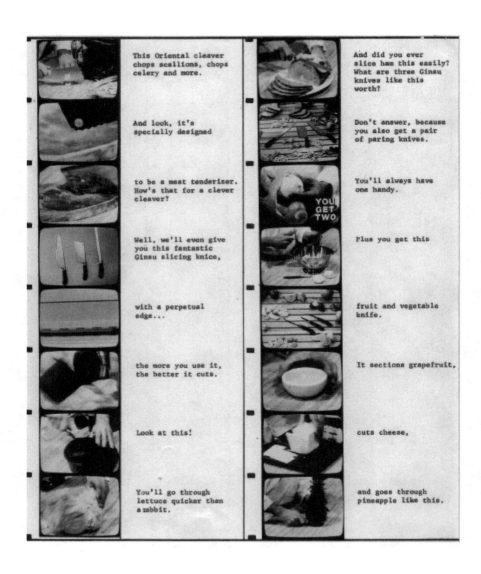

This Oriental cleaver chops scallions, chops celery and more.

And look, it's specially designed

to be a meat tenderizer. How's that for a clever cleaver?

Well, we'll even give you this fantastic Ginsu slicing knice,

with a perpetual edge...

the more you use it, the better it cuts.

Look at this!

You'll go through lettuce quicker than a rabbit.

And did you ever slice ham this easily? What are three Ginsu knives like this worth?

Don't answer, because you also get a pair of paring knives.

You'll always have one handy.

YOU GET TWO

Plus you get this

fruit and vegetable knife.

It sections grapefruit,

cuts cheese,

and goes through pineapple like this.

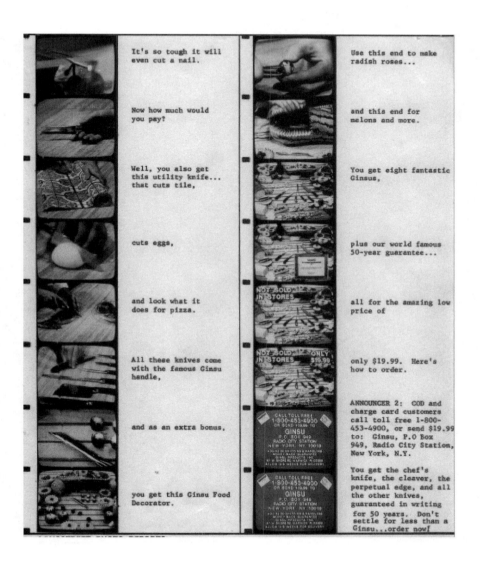

It's so tough it will even cut a nail.

Now how much would you pay?

Well, you also get this utility knife... that cuts tile,

cuts eggs,

and look what it does for pizza.

All these knives come with the famous Ginsu handle,

and as an extra bonus,

you get this Ginsu Food Decorator.

Use this end to make radish roses...

and this end for melons and more.

You get eight fantastic Ginsus,

plus our world famous 50-year guarantee...

all for the amazing low price of

only $19.99. Here's how to order.

ANNOUNCER 2: COD and charge card customers call toll free 1-800-453-4900, or send $19.99 to: Ginsu, P.O Box 949, Radio City Station, New York, N.Y.

You get the chef's knife, the cleaver, the perpetual edge, and all the other knives, guaranteed in writing for 50 years. Don't settle for less than a Ginsu...order now!

Never Settle for What People Tell You

Barry

After famous actor and dancer Fred Astaire's first screen test, a 1933 memo from the MGM testing director said, "Can't act. Slightly balding and can dance a little."

Walt Disney was fired by a newspaper because he "lacked imagination." He also went bankrupt several times before he started Disney.

It's never a good idea to settle for what people tell you because they could be misinformed, unintentionally misleading you, or just plain lying. It's always a good idea to double-check what is being told to you. Remember this the next time you're faced with an obstacle such as getting an appointment or closing a sale.

If you don't like what you are hearing, find a way around it. Here's how.

Ed

Whenever I have a problem shopping, I never settle for what a clerk tells me. I always ask for the manager (I know from experience that clerks are not empowered to solve my problem). I explain my complaint and inform him that I am an important stockholder via mutual funds. He has no idea how many shares I own. Then, most importantly, I tell him what I want to fix the problem. I never allow him to think about a solution. I have one in mind and I make it easy for them to make a decision. I could devote several chapters on the many times I've used this technique successfully, but in the interest of saving trees, here are two:

1. My favorite Hotel in New York City.

My favorite because it has great accommodations, great location (midtown), and, most importantly, someone there always screws up! My last visit was right in the middle of writing this book. I checked in for a two-night stay, and when I opened the door to the room I smelled cigarette smoke. I had asked for a no smoking room. Next, the room safe wouldn't work. I called the front desk to deodorize the room and fix the safe. They didn't. The next day they forgot to give me the wake-up call I had asked for. "Wonderful," I thought, "at least these guys are consistent." Because all of my problems were not of a significant nature, I didn't let it spoil my weekend.

When I checked out, I knew the question was coming.

"So, how did you enjoy your stay?" asked the checkout clerk.

"I didn't," I answered.

The desk clerk asked me for the details. After I explained my complaints, the desk clerk apologized and promised to do better on my next visit.

At that point most people would just leave.

"That's not good enough," I said and I asked to speak to the manager.

The manager came over to see what the problem was. When I explained the complaints again, he asked, "What can we do to rectify this and make you happy?"

Bingo!

I said, "I would like two free nights on my next visit to make up for this experience." He agreed!

If I had settled for what they first told me, I would have been on my way home without a two-night voucher in my pocket.

Does this always happen? No. They don't screw up every time, and I don't always get what I want (sometimes I get a free dinner), but they screw up enough so that it makes the few minutes of complaining worthwhile.

2. My favorite airline (actually *any* airline, because they all screw up).

I try to use any opportunity I can, any screw-up on the part of the airlines, to upgrade my seat from coach to first class. Sometimes, I impress even myself and get free travel. The mistake many people make when dealing with the airlines is that they lose control by losing their temper. It never works! Remain calm.

It's much more to your advantage to have them say, " I appreciate your being so calm about this." It makes the person dealing with your problem that much more willing to go beyond the limits to get you what you want. There is truth to the old line your mother told you, "You catch more flies with honey." It's impossible to list the many ways an airline can screw up. There are so many. But whenever you catch them in error—that is, lost bags, delays (not weather), poor customer service, bad attitude from employees—you need to ask for a supervisor and do the drill—that is, good customer, loyal to the airline in a time when customer loyalty is limited to their options or price.

If they don't ask the magic question, "What can I do to make this right?" speak up and say, "This is what I am looking for to make it right." I always try to ask for things that don't cost the airline money. The airline has plenty of empty seats, so giving me a free ticket is not a big deal. It will push my travel dates anyway and the airline won't take the ticket unless there are open seats. Also, a first-class upgrade is a no-brainer. If there is room, it's yours. On the subject of first class, I ask for upgrades even when the airlines do it right, as I explain in the Ginsuism "always ask."

Here's an example of a situation that could have cost us millions, but we didn't settle for what people told us.

Ed

Each week we were taking in between 20,000 and 50,000 checks totaling between $400,000 and $1 million for various products such as Ginsu and Armourcote cookware. Well, the banks loved the money we were depositing, but hated the work involved in processing all those checks. We would get supermarket shopping bags and fill them with checks and take them to the bank. The tellers would groan when our people showed up at the bank, as they were responsible for balancing the deposit. That meant they had to count every check deposited. So, in an effort to build good customer relations, the bank told us that it would charge us a fee of 5 cents per check deposited, and, because almost all of our checks were from out of state, a hold would be put on monies collected from those checks for two weeks, therefore tying up our cash flow. This would certainly affect our fragile profit margin, as we were probably only making 50 cents on each product sale at that time, and the bank would now be getting 10 percent of our profits. Barry wouldn't settle for what the bank people were telling him. He did research on this situation. He scoured the federal and state regulations and discovered that the Federal Reserve had just passed a new law allowing corporations to open corporate savings accounts. These new savings accounts mandated that interest be paid from the day of deposit and all funds be considered collected on the day of deposit. Furthermore, the law stated that no fee could be charged for deposits in these types of accounts.

We immediately started putting the new law to work for us. We started depositing all the shopping bags' of checks into our new corporate savings account. We not only saved the 5 cents fee per check, but we earned 4 percent interest from the day of deposit and got immediate use of the money by calling the bank and making a phone transfer to our checking account the next day. What a boon it was to our business to have all the deposited funds available to us the next day. It instantly increased our cash flow and our credit standing because we could pay all our bills sooner. Now, we had the bank by the "vaults." They learned a lesson, and we had another rule to live by: never settle for what people tell you.

Here's another example:

When we first opened PriMedia, we rented space in a very attractive new building. The area we occupied was arranged so that everyone except the receptionist had a private office. The building was shaped like an X and was two stories high. We signed a five-year lease and everything was going along fine for three years, and then the landlord went bankrupt. Without our knowledge, an auction was held and the building was sold. Shortly thereafter we received a certified letter from the new landlord telling us that as per paragraphs 14 and 18, our lease was terminated and we had until the end of the month to vacate the premises. Most of the tenants were up in arms, but by the end of the month they had meekly moved out of the building. To us, the letter said it's "time to relocate," but we took that to mean it's "time to negotiate." We ended up staying there many more months and reached a settlement with the new landlord. A confidentiality statement prevents us from discussing the details; however, it forced us to look for another location, which ended up being an extremely valuable building at a fantastic discounted price that is now worth many times more than its cost. I bought the building and PriMedia still occupies it today.

People are afraid of legal contracts and official seals and documents. We are not lemmings in our society. If we had listened to what they told us in this instance, we would have probably gone out of business.

People will almost always tell you what is most convenient for and best for them. Remember, "never settle for what people tell you."

There's No Red Cross Flag Flying Over This Building

Barry

We sold more than 40 products, garnering $500 million in sales over 10 years and pioneered the use of credit cards and 800 numbers on TV. At one point we were spending more than Coca-Cola and a little less than AT&T on TV advertising, buying more than $5 million per quarter while taking in $1 million per week. All these dollar figures are here for a reason: to remind you that the whole purpose of starting a business is to make money and be profitable. If you ain't making money, you ain't in business.

The Wisdom of Ginsu

After the sale of our company, and a brief retirement, we opened up PriMedia. Our mission statement was to operate as a "virtual" advertising agency whose primary focus was to use the knowledge we had gained negotiating low rates on multimillion-dollar television direct response schedules and our extensive direct response media knowledge to the benefit of more traditional clients.

As soon as we started the business, the calls began pouring in.

"I've got this great product," or "I've got this great idea. You just have to see it! It's the next Ginsu, I know it!"

For a while we met with many would-be inventors and promising millionaires. Nothing ever developed. Lots of time wasted. We did meet many interesting people, but we didn't earn any money. Eventually it became clear to us that it was time to take the Red Cross flag down from on top of our building. It must have been up there flying pretty high. Why else would everyone come in looking for free help! With the flag down, we started charging for an initial consultation and the calls dwindled down from way too many generating zero income to a manageable number generating a nice steady income. I guess a lot of the initial "tire kickers" never saw an idea they wouldn't be very comfortable investing our time and money in! When it came to media buying, we were in the same exact scenario. We would get calls asking us to do extensive media plans on a "spec" (speculative) basis. These plans were exacting in detail. They contained budgets, allocation of money by media, specific stations, and an overall reach and frequency. Done correctly, they took many hours and many people to prepare. When they were completed, the only thing left for us to do was to pull the trigger and call the order into the various media. Can you guess what happened? Most of the initial plans we prepared never materialized.

The people calling us were on fishing expeditions, looking for free advice, and we were giving it to them. No charge. Now we charge upfront for a media plan and deduct the cost of the plan should the buy be placed by PriMedia. If not, we at least have been paid for the time and effort expended. Of course there are other elements to our strategy here that we will never reveal (see Chapter 7 for more on keeping your secrets to yourself).

Are there times when you should be charitable? Yes, to your existing client base and customers. After all, they are your lifeblood, and you don't want to nickel and dime them to death. This Ginsuism is primarily designed to help you understand that there are people out there who are looking for a free ride. With PriMedia's current client base, based on the relationship the companies have built with each other, they nurture them, give them advice, and help them grow their businesses in many ways, some of which do not provide revenue each and every time they do it. This is in recognition of the big picture and recognition by both parties of the benefits of a long-term relationship. In the long run, they retain their business and loyalty, keep the clients happy, and earn a fair and reasonable profit, relative to the cost-saving and value-added benefits they bring to the table. You've heard about being able to see the big picture clearly. Well, PriMedia's story is a good example.

Remember that you are in a profit business and you are not a charity. You are not the Red Cross. Don't give away ideas or advice for free. Charge for them.

Ed

Early in my career I remember being at a cocktail party where there was a prominent local interior decorator. One woman went up to the decorator, introduced herself, and said, "I have this burgundy leather couch with a gray rug in my family room. What would you recommend for the color of the drapes?"

The decorator excused himself and walked away. A few minutes later I saw the woman carefully navigate over to where he was and again ask the same question.

This time the decorator spoke and said, "I'm sorry. I don't work on weekends, but if you like, here's my card. Please call my office to make an appointment."

The Wisdom of Ginsu

I love it! What he is really saying, in a nice way is, "I worked hard to get where I am today. I have a talent and if you want it, you have to pay for it!"

Doctors at cocktail parties or elsewhere say the same thing when asked, "Hey Doc, what's this?"

"Could be any one of a number of things," the doctor says. "Why don't you call my office and make an appointment?"

Do you think medical school was free? Profit is not an ugly word, and I never, I mean *never*, apologize for making one. Without profit there is no incentive. No incentive, no motivation.

Look what happened to communism. I remember reading about a reporter who went to Moscow before the breakup of the Soviet Union. He very much wanted to dine in a Russian restaurant and try the local cuisine. One night he decided to try one of the places recommended to him near his hotel. When he went in, there were just a few tables occupied. After he was seated he noticed the wait staff congregated in a corner of the restaurant smoking and chatting away. Expecting to get some prompt service because they were not busy, he in fact waited more than 40 minutes for someone to come to his table to take his order. It took another hour for the food to arrive and 30 minutes for the check. Two hours and 10 minutes for the entire pathetic experience. The next day he told his Russian friend who recommended the restaurant about his ordeal.

His friend laughed and said, "You forget, this is not the USA. Here in Russia all the waiters and waitresses make the same pay and tipping is not allowed."

No incentive, no motivation. It just didn't matter if he was a happy diner or not. Think motivation and incentive are not important? Try this: the next time you are in a restaurant in this country, try telling the waiter or waitress before you order that he or she is not getting a tip. Let me know what kind of service you get.

Once you make some money, remember that the primary purpose of going into business is to make a lot of money and to keep as much of it as possible. If you don't own a business, it's part of your job and in your own best interest to protect your employer from giving away your next raise unnecessarily. Constantly remind yourself that as a for-profit firm, "there's no Red Cross flag flying over this building."

Solid Stainless Steel

13

Not Making a Mistake Is a Big Mistake

Barry

In fact, not making a mistake might be the biggest mistake you *never* make!

You've heard it said by successful entrepreneurs over and over again: "I'm not an overnight success. I just learned from my mistakes." The truth is that very few "success stories" happen on the first try. In fact, if you check into it, I'm willing to bet that the people behind some of the biggest success stories have previously experienced some of the biggest failures. Having never experienced failure or made a mistake, how prepared are you to deal with an emergency or crisis situation? Answer: not very. Don't get us wrong, we both hate to lose and love to win. But we've learned to accept and even welcome failure as an opportunity to learn and solve a puzzle that will eventually make us successful. And because we've failed before, we know what to look for and how to handle similar situations when they arise again, which they invariably do.

That said, check out this doozy of a mistake. Boy did we lose—and learn—a lot from this one!

In 1979 one of the stations that produced many orders for us was Ted Turner's WTBS in Atlanta. WTBS had transformed itself from a local Atlanta station to a *superstation* and was one of the first stations to broadcast via satellite. In order to receive satellite stations in those days most people had to have a 10-foot dish antenna on their roofs or in their backyards.

Back then, cable TV was in its infancy and, in order for WTBS to produce advertising revenue, it had to prove to large national advertisers that it had viewers. Until that time, Ted Turner in his genius allowed WTBS to do per inquiry product advertising. WTBS would simply allow direct response advertisers like us to take the unsold advertising slots on the station and run our commercials. Instead of paying a fixed rate for the spots we had to pay WTBS 30 percent of the retail selling price of the product. This ensured WTBS that any unsold air time produced some revenue. The only stipulation that the station had was that the product first be demonstrated as being able to generate orders on other stations. This was another clever Turner idea, ensuring him a successful product. For every unit we sold at $10 we gave WTBS $3. This guaranteed us a profit (by fixing our advertising expense) and created revenue for his startup enterprise. At that time WTBS did not subscribe to the rating services, so in an attempt to convince the big buck advertisers that people from all over the country were indeed watching WTBS, he tried to sell them air time based on the fact that the station had sold so many Ginsus in Chicago, Cleveland, Dallas, and so forth. People must be watching if they bought Ginsus from his station! How else could they have ordered a Ginsu? Clever! At 2,000 sets of knives a week at a guaranteed profit for us, WTBS was certainly a situation we liked. No risk, all reward.

One day our controller came to us and said, "Ted Turner wants you to loan him $100,000."

Not Making a Mistake Is a Big Mistake

Ed

I almost choked on the sandwich I was eating. Now, $100,000 might not seem like a lot these days, but in 1979 it was a lot of money. Furthermore, the only thing we really knew about Ted Turner was that he was somewhat of a maverick; that he had attended our local prestigious Ivy League college, Brown University; that he owned WTBS; and that he had recently won the America's Cup in Newport. We asked our controller what he wanted the money for and he laughed as he said, "He wants to start a 24-hour news station on the satellite."

"Who's going to watch it"? I asked.

"Probably nobody," came the reply from Barry.

We told him we'd kick the idea around.

I said, "Listen, Barry, I'm a former broadcaster and this is one lousy idea! Who the heck will watch news 24 hours a day?"

It really was a crazy idea. We thought Turner was nuts, but still we didn't want to ruin the great deal we had with WTBS. After some lively discussion between us we figured it would be okay if WTBS guaranteed the loan against future orders; after all, we were paying them $6,000 a week anyway. We would be able to recover the money in 12 or 13 weeks.

Turner's people responded with, "No deal: it's a straight loan, no guarantees, no nothing." Because we already thought he was crazy to do this news idea, we declined.

Well, let me tell you, we sure prejudged. We never asked if he had any research to back him up. We never asked how many homes would be reached. We never even asked why he thought it was a good idea. We were sure that in this instance we were smarter than Ted Turner. Not!

Barry

To show you what prejudging can do to you, I have to tell you what followed. When our next product, Armourcote cookware, was ready for airing WTBS wouldn't accept it. The company had turned cold to us. That probably cost us $250,000 in lost profits. It was the same with our next product, which sold like crazy everywhere but never aired on WTBS. Plus, to add insult to injury, Turner's 24-hour news channel is now called CNN. Making that mistake was costly, but it taught us a valuable lesson: never prejudge!

And if you ever happen to meet us and see us going through our daily ritual of pounding our heads against the wall and yelling at each other, "Stupid, Stupid, Stupid!" you'll know why we're doing it.

Here's another mistake we made. To this day, I still shake my head over the fact that we routinely charged $9.95 and $19.95 for our products, instead of asking for $9.99 and $19.99. We seriously doubt whether a single customer who ordered one of our products would have changed his mind if we had asked for 4 cents more. With millions of units sold, that sure cost us a bit of change. In fact, on Ginsu alone we would have earned about $100,000 more.

Want more Ed and Barry blunders? After the sale of our company, we consulted for a while, and we used the money we'd made to do a little speculative investing. We invested in cattle whose beef, we later found out, was being rejected even by the people who make hot dogs. We put money into oil and gas wells. The last we heard they were pumping out more than a million barrels a day—of dust.

It wasn't until years later when we were much more investor-savvy that we put a ton of money into a bunch of companies that we knew would go through the roof: Internet stocks. We were even richer for about three weeks, and then the bubble burst. By the way, if any of you are interested, I can let you have cheap all our shares of *www.toiletpaper.com*. It was an apt name, because that's what we've been using our shares of stock for since.

Ed

Then in 1990, after a few years of retirement, we went on to found PriMedia, a national media buying and marketing agency that is still around today. That was not a mistake! Thirty years later, Barry and I were still together, right up to the day he retired. And today, our friendship is stronger than ever.

Moral of the story? We were lucky enough to meet each other, make money, keep our friendship, and come up with one of the most recognized products in television history, but not lucky enough to know how to invest it well. As much as we learned and as well as we did—nobody's perfect—you're going to make mistakes. We sure did.

Not Making a Mistake Is a Big Mistake

However, be thankful for those mistakes because they will teach you more than you ever thought you'd need to know. When you feel that you have made a mistake, write it down. Keep a journal of your mistakes. Look at it from time to time and analyze the errors that you made. See if you could have done a better job by thinking about ways that you could have acted differently, and what the outcome might have been. This kind of mental gymnastics will help you to think differently. Remember, great entrepreneurs seem to always learn from their mistakes and find ways not to repeat them.

Also, never prejudge a situation. Do your due diligence. Please, find out all the facts. Investigate the situation, even if you think it doesn't make sense or you think it's crazy!

In closing, don't be afraid to make a mistake. Mistakes, as painful as they can be, do actually help you learn and grow.

Someone wrote a great line about business and mistakes: "I think the worst problem in business is having a boss who's stubborn, pig-headed, and refuses to admit mistakes: especially if you're self-employed."

Remember, every misstep you take in your career or personal life can teach you a valuable lesson that you can use to go to the next level or to prevent future misfortune. Without mistakes, nothing is really learned, and learning is the key to entrepreneurial and personal success. "Not making a mistake is a big mistake"—maybe the biggest you never make.

When You Ask Someone a Question, Wait for the Answer!

Barry

How many times have you said the wrong thing, simply because you were too impatient to wait for an answer and too sure of yourself and your own brilliance to actually listen to what the person had to say? I can't tell you how many times I've had people give me the answers to the questions they asked me, without giving me a chance to answer. And, when they do that, it always ends up to my advantage, or really ticks me off. Either way, my own reaction is enough for me pass this Ginsuism on to you. I don't care how brilliant or incredible you think your idea is or what you have to say sounds to you; if it's that good now, it will still be good when the other person finishes, so jot it down. Don't have anything to write on? Always bring a notebook and pen with you, no matter who you are, or how important you think you are. This will not only help you not interrupt, but you'll be amazed at the reaction when you send your client a written summary of the meeting that is accurate and shows that you were listening. Want to know why? Because not many people do it anymore (listen or take notes). That's right: something that seems to be common sense and that everyone used to do now makes you stand out from your competitors! Common courtesy and common sense: put them together and it's quite the winning combination.

Ever hear about salespeople who talk themselves into a sale then talk their way out of it? They ask, "How much would you be willing to pay?" Then before the customer can answer, they ask, "How about this?"

When this happens to me, I think to myself, "Thanks, I was willing to pay more."

If the salesperson names a price that is higher than I'm willing to pay, at least I know where I stand and can do some serious bargaining.

I like to think of these people as people who just cannot get enough of the sound of their own voice and who talk away profits.

Most times when someone speaks instead of listening, he is providing you with ammunition that can be used against him.

A person will come to our office and spend half an hour with a fancy presentation and when he is done ask, "Well, what do you think?"

Now, we've just spent a half hour listening to something that we have never before seen or heard. We have probably absorbed about 10 percent of the presentation, and our mental computer is still processing the rest of the information. Undoubtedly we have many questions to ask, but before we can utter a word the presenter will say something such as, "I know you gentlemen are very busy and I've taken up a lot of your time, and I know that these are difficult times for your business but, etc."

Let's see now. We had allotted one hour for this, so we have 30 minutes left and business is great. The presenter, by not waiting for us to think and reply, has already given us two objections if we want to get rid of him or her. Then if we try and save this person by saying, "No problem, we've got some time," invariably this type of person will do it again by saying something such as this: "I know you gentlemen have been around for a long time, so when I said that our product was unique I realize that you've probably seen similar products before and my statement might be a bit of an exaggeration, but...."

Of course, we've probably never seen anything like it before, but we now realize they have competition. Now I have been provided with three objections. Thanks. I might also be thinking, "What else was said that might just border on the truth?" This presentation was doomed before it began. Not because of the product, but because the presenter loved the sound of his or her own voice and just would not shut up!

Here's what should have happened.

Ed

I remember a Xerox sales training course I attended when I was in radio. You waited for the objection, listened, and repeated the objection back to the client, then overcame the objection. Here's what it sounds like.

You finish your presentation and then say, "Okay, that concludes my presentation. Any questions?" Now you wait and keep your mouth shut.

Someone says, "That's great, but I simply cannot afford to make this kind of purchase."

Now you repeat the objection. You say, "I just want to make sure I understand. You are concerned about the price and your ability to afford this. Is this correct?"

The person replies yes.

Now you ask, "Is that your only concern? Would you make the purchase if you could afford it?"

If the client says yes, you have isolated the objection. Now you overcome it.

"Mr. Client, if I were able to find a way to solve that problem, then would you be willing to make the purchase?"

You either solve the problem right there if you have the answer or you say, "Let me work on that and I will get back to you." Don't make objections for yourself. You will get your fair share. Believe me!

Barry

Another line we hate hearing is, "I know what you're thinking." It is absolutely amazing how many mind readers we've come in contact with over the years. How all these people thought they knew what we were thinking boggles the mind.

Here's an example: we say, "We've got a little problem with something you said."

The reply is, "I know what you're thinking."

That person is not even sure of what we were thinking, but we are about to be told anyway. "You're thinking about points A, B, C, and D, right?" Wrong, Captain Clairvoyant.

Actually we were thinking about point E, but now we have doubts about A,B,C, and D. "Thanks for the info, didn't think of that." Out of 1,000 times, he or she might be right once. I love it.

Some of you may have been in the military. We were, and we were warned to "never volunteer for anything."

Don't volunteer answers to questions that you ask. Waiting for an answer will not only steer you in the right direction, but at times it will provide you with an answer to your question, and it may also tell you something about the person you are dealing with. An exaggeration of this is if you ask the question, "Is the sky blue?"

The answer you might get is, "No, it's pink and orange and yellow." That answer will give you a hint as to the type of personality you are dealing with.

If the answer is, "It's black!" well, you're probably going to have to work much harder with this type of personality.

Ed

Here's a great example and it just happened this year. My office copy machine was out of date and, as a result, was in constant need of repair. Fortunately we had a great service contract so all of the repairs were free. The service tech was almost invited to our Christmas party because he was over so often and knew everyone in the office. After a while it became an irritant to us, so we asked the company that sold it to us to give us a price on a new one. Because this was the same company that was servicing the machine via the service contract, we were sure company reps would be receptive to giving us a really good deal because it must be costing the company money to keep coming out to the office. Guess what? Saving money on the service calls was only moderately interesting to them. They gave us a meager discount and we walked.

We then contacted another company. Now enter a real salesperson. This guy shows up with a machine that looks like the transporter on the Starship Enterprise. He demonstrates the machine, hits us with the price, and we say, "Can't afford that."

He says, "No problem, I will show you how to get this machine free!"

Now he has my attention. He asks to visit the accounting department to crunch some numbers, leaves, and returns with the following analysis.

"Ed, the machine I want to sell you not only replaces the copy machine, but each printer in every office. Based on the amount of copies you made last year at 4 cents vs. my machine at 2 cents, plus the cost of all your black-and-white and color cartridges, your savings will be enough to cover the cost of the lease on the machine. It's like getting it for free! When shall I deliver it?"

Done!

God gave you two ears and only one mouth; do the math.

"When you ask a question, wait for the answer!" Remember, ask the question, sit back, relax, and wait for the answer. Listen to it, absorb it, and make sure you understand it before you respond.

Sometimes Smart People Do Stupid Things!

Ed

In the movie *Forrest Gump*, Forrest says, "Stupid is as stupid does."

In my business (ad agency), sales managers of radio and TV stations are always asking me to send them the names of good salespeople.

"Good ones are in short supply," they say. They feel that, because we have so many sales reps calling on us at the agency, perhaps we know and can refer one or two candidates. That sometimes is a challenge because I can honestly say that there is a huge difference in the sales reps from when I was in the business (1969 to 1975) to the reps of today. Which is why I get so many requests for referrals. In fact, I would go as far to say that almost all salespeople today, regardless of what industry they work in, are very different.

Let me explain. Back in my day (early 1970s), having a sales job open up at a radio or TV station was a big deal, let alone actually landing one. These jobs were considered prestigious and the industry paid good money. My last sales job in TV paid $42,000 in 1975 dollars. Everyone worked hard, made good money, and, most importantly, paid attention to the basics that we speak about in this book. Basics such as returning phone calls and showing up on time for appointments. We remembered we were in the client service business, took clients to lunch, and often stopped by their businesses to say hello or to see how things were progressing. Our job was to grow their business. The logic being that if our advertising increased sales, they would spend more money with us. More money meant more commissions. My personal philosophy in servicing my client list was to be in their faces and become a partner in growing their businesses. I would learn as much as I could about their businesses by reading and asking lots of questions. It worked for me. I also never made the client feel as if I owned the station by making it difficult to get things done. To them, the clients, I was their advocate. It was up to me to find a way to get their requests done.

I remember an old boss of mine who said, "Ed, you do your best selling on the inside."

I fought for my clients inside the station. If a lower rate on some programming was the difference between my getting the sale or not, I would do battle inside and try to make the sale with my boss. My clients always knew this.

Today, many salespeople say, "I can't do that. No way, sorry."

They give all of these reasons they can't do something before checking to see if they can! I see this every day. I don't want to hear problems; I have enough of my own. I want solutions. I want a salesperson. Someone who can sell and make things happen. I want someone to say, "Ed, let me check into this and I'll get right back to you." Or "Ed, I'll try and find a way to get you what you want."

Sometimes Smart People Do Stupid Things!

Not the autopilot brainless phrases I usually get. Why do you think they call it *sales* instead of *order taking*? Honestly, most of these salespeople can be replaced with an answering machine or voice mail. Just record all of the things you can't do, tell your clients all of the problems you have, and let them push buttons. Remember, while you are out there complaining and whining and feeling sorry for yourself or even basking in your "holier than thou" attitude, someone else out there may be cleaning your clock by selling, making things happen, turning problems into opportunities, and *making money*!

ThoughI could probably write a separate book on this subject alone, I will just give you three classic stories. Read on and try to remember you are not entering the twilight zone, and this is not *Candid Camera*. This is real life.

Case in point #1: A saleswoman in one of our markets who works for a prominent media company and is considered the "top dog." She has the biggest list of accounts, including our agency, and I would suspect makes big money (easily six figures, a large percentage of which is derived from sales she gets from us). Here's what happened. A business associate had asked me to try and get some of the TV and radio stations to buy ads in a charitable scholarship program book (a very common practice in this particular market). Every single one of the radio and TV stations purchased ads, without hesitation, from a full page costing $250 down to a business card ad for $25. Everyone except, guess who? When I sent the e-mail request to everyone, I stated the request and charity and indicated that they could participate for a little as $25. Obviously I said that I would appreciate their help.

Her reply to me was, "No! I give my money to a different local charity."

I couldn't believe it! I was so beside myself when I read her e-mail reply that I didn't know what to do for days. How could anyone be so out of touch? I wasn't asking her personally; I was asking for her company to take an ad out. She didn't even have the common sense to take it to her boss for some direction. Here she is, taking more than half a million dollars of business out of our agency, earning a solid commission, and she refuses a $25 request. Because this woman or her company has never given me as much as a bus token, or invited me to lunch, I guess it was foolish of me to think they would cough up $25 for charity.

You know the line "the apple doesn't fall far from the tree" when referring to children mirroring their parents' behavior or growing up to be just like their parents? This is sometimes painfully true of companies. I've learned that the employee is sometimes the apple and the tree is the boss or company. Most often, if you receive bad service or a bad attitude, the manager or owner is the same way. How else could it be otherwise? Bad attitude in a waitress usually means someone at the top condones this behavior, or it would stop. Sales reps not giving good service means some boss has taught them this way or condones it also. Not every time, but often. Look around. You'll spot it.

Anyway, when I complained to the woman's boss, he finally invited me to lunch. Wow! He agreed it was silly and stupid behavior on the part of his rep and promised to correct it. Good! When I asked him how he likes living in the state, he replied, "What do you mean? I've lived here for six years." I was astonished. He had been in Rhode Island for six years and had never bothered to come out and meet one of his biggest clients, until a problem popped up. Guess that apple didn't fall too far….

Case in point #2: A local radio station was looking for our business and the sales rep invited me and one of my buyers to lunch with her and the general manager of the station. We met at a local restaurant and listened to them hawk their station and the importance of reaching their target audience. I was already sold on the idea but listened and suggested that a good candidate to try on their station would be one of our clients: the family-owned TASCA Automotive Group, one of the most respected automotive groups in the country. Our lunch host was excited. I even suggested that we try it for a year with a good dollar commitment and give the morning show host a car to drive around in so he could talk about his experiences. They promised they would get us a proposal fast. We thanked them for lunch and left. That was three years ago. I'm still waiting for the proposal. Think the radio business has the exclusive on this problem? Think again. It's everywhere and it's getting worse. I jokingly say to some of my buyers in trying to understand this mentality, "Guess they must have a line of clients wrapped around their building waiting to give them money."

Case in point #3: This is a story about a radio station in Boston, approximately 50 miles away, or an hour drive from where I am in Rhode Island. We agreed to lunch with one of the station representatives who wanted to bring along his boss. His boss wanted to meet me and thank me for the business we had just placed on the station. So far so good, right? But wait! We agreed on a day and the time was set for noon at my office. That day 12:15 came, and nothing. I assume when meeting people from Boston that they might be 15 to 20 minutes late because of the traffic and the controversial "Big Dig" (Massachusetts's multibillion dollar attempt to reroute traffic in and around Boston), which has been going on for years. While I assume someone from Boston will almost never be on time, I do expect and usually get a phone call saying, "We'll be late." This time, nothing. Nothing at 12:30, and again at 12:45, nothing. Now, not only am I hungry, but I'm getting angry. Finally, at 1 p.m., bingo, I get the call.

The rep says, "Ed, I left Boston late. I'm halfway to your office and am turning around and going back to the station. The traffic is awful. Can we reschedule?"

What? I couldn't conceive of treating my clients this way and expecting to keep their business. What the hell are these people thinking? Or perhaps they are not thinking at all.

More often than you would think, I get salespeople in my office who routinely leave money on the table. How? They don't ask for the order! In the media business we often have to meet a cost per rating point. This is a method of determining how efficient a station is in reaching the audience you need to meet your client's goal and the price it charges for the commercial time to achieve that goal. When one station has a CPP (cost per rating point) that is higher in cost than the others in the market, we ask if the rep can lower the price of

139

the spots or add free spots to reduce the overall cost, or we'll have to eliminate the station from the buy.

When a station inquires, "Am I on this buy?"

We sometimes respond by saying, "Your CPP is too high. You are not competitive and we may have to eliminate your station."

Incredible as it may seem, we get many salespeople (or should I say *order takers*) who say, "Okay, let me know when the next buy is coming up."

What a real salesperson would or should say is, "What can I do to get on this buy and get some of your business?"

In other words, let's make something happen. "What do you need to make it work, Ed?"

Instead, the rep leaves the building. No order in hand. The money goes to someone else and we scratch our heads in bewilderment. True, sometimes there isn't any room for negotiation. Perhaps a station is sold out and the salesperson just cannot do anything to accommodate your request. This I understand. My problem is that salespeople don't ask and they don't try. If the business is there, then fine. If not, they don't want to work for it. They just expect it. These people have a warped sense of entitlement.

Remember, the only thing you are entitled to in the sales business is to make a commission when you make a sale. That's it!

Okay, some of these examples seem hard to believe and you might be saying to yourself right now, "I don't do that! That's not how I do business. These stories are extreme."

Well, perhaps they are. But there is a lot of gray area between these stories and, being the best salesperson you can be, and I'll bet most of us at one time or another fall somewhere in the middle. The sad part is, some of you are still there. And some of you just don't know that you're there.

Remember, there are three types of people:
1. People who know.
2. People who don't know.
3. People who don't know enough to know they don't know.

Sometimes Smart People Do Stupid Things!

Are you one of the ones who doesn't know enough to know you don't know? Think about it. Try to evaluate your performance before someone else does and lets you go or, worse, lets you go...out of business.

In Chapter 9 we talk about the importance of returning phone calls, but until everyone gets on the same page, there are some things that you should be doing. It's called put your pride aside and keep calling someone until you get a response. I remember reading a story about an advertising executive in Los Angeles who called the Disney people every day for one year to try and get their advertising business. Finally he got an appointment to see them, and eventually he got the account. So, you see, as smart as this guy was for calling every single day, it would have been very easy not to by telling himself that it was a waste of time. Yet, if he had not called the client every day for a year, that would have to be classified as a really stupid thing to do. Why? Because if he hadn't, it would have cost him an account worth tens of millions of dollars, just to save himself about two minutes a day; a real no-brainer.

In the movie *Wall Street*, Charlie Sheen plays the part of a stockbroker who calls a potential client every day for an appointment. Finally, when they meet the client says, "They should put your picture in the dictionary under persistence." If you want someone's business, be prepared to earn it. Don't assume that if someone doesn't return your call the first few times that it's a dead issue. Keep trying until you hear the words yourself. Don't assume.

We all have had experiences with contractors or anyone doing work on our houses or apartments. Apart from the many horror stories, the common thread is that they never show up or call back. We think nothing of calling them a few hundred times to make sure they come, right? After we nail them on the phone, they say, "I've been meaning to call you but it's been crazy." The important point is, we eventually get them to show up! But in business after a few calls not returned, we say, "They must not be interested. If they were, they would have called back." The contractor is interested, but perhaps not very good at managing his or her business. The same could be true here also. Perhaps he or she has a contractor's mentality in a business that requires a diplomat's touch. And finally, one last telling tale of a normally smart person doing a very stupid thing:

His name was Harry and he had enjoyed a very long and somewhat successful career as an on-air personality and sales rep for a local radio station. Of course, one day the inevitable happened, and he was laid off. Within a few weeks he went to work for an agency he had done business with and was asked to go along on a sales pitch. He was also asked to keep his mouth shut and listen, which he did, flawlessly, during a crucial presentation of a six-figure TV campaign to a major drugstore chain. Despite the brilliance of the campaign and to Harry's surprise, the major drugstore chain said no to the campaign. The agency owner, having invested quite a bit of time and money in developing the campaign, and believing in the quality of the work, immediately got on the phone and set up an appointment with the first drugstore chain's main competitor. Harry was again invited along to observe, and he sat silently in awe once again as the agency head presented the campaign better than any he had ever pitched before.

The second drugstore chain was eating it up and wanted to start the campaign as soon as possible. As the agency pitch team began to close the sale by shaking hands with the client's representatives on their way out the door, Harry began to chuckle. The president/CEO of the drugstore chain asked him what he found so amusing and Harry replied, "Oh, nothing. I'm just amazed at how much you loved this campaign. When we showed it to DrugsR'Us (alias for competitive drug company's name) yesterday, they hated it!" Needless to say, the agency lost the sale, and Harry lost his job soon thereafter.

No matter how smart you are, you're capable of doing some really stupid things. Recognize this and be ready to correct it. Sometimes it can be the only difference between success and failure.

It's great to know, and it's okay to not know, but you don't ever want to be the person who doesn't know you don't know. You can't be good at everything, so accept it and act accordingly. After all, you're a smart person, so why continue to do stupid things?

Sometimes Smart People Do Stupid Things!

And remember, no matter how smart you think you are, "sometimes smart people do stupid things!"

When You Help Other People, You Help Yourself

Ed

There are two sure ways to get your boss's job. One way is to get him or her fired. The other is to get him or her promoted. The first way has risks. What if your attempt to get your boss fired backfires? You could be the person with a one-way ticket out the door. We are big proponents of the second method. A friend of mine who was second in command of a radio station constantly searched the job postings of broadcast publications, circled the ones he thought his boss would be a good fit for, and put them on his desk. It was humorous of course, but not too far off base. The only way he could get that job was for his boss to leave. By helping him, he'd be helping himself!

145

The Wisdom of Ginsu

Barry

Throughout our careers we have gone out of our way many times to help people get promoted, get hired, or just get ahead. Not only is it a satisfying experience to see someone you've helped make it big, or land back on his feet, but as the old saying goes, "what goes around, comes around." There was a time a few years back when we got a call from someone in the radio business who we had known for many years. Greg was an extremely hard worker and he was the general manager of a local radio station. It was a position he had worked 20 years to achieve. He called the office one day and said in a crestfallen voice that his employment had just been terminated. He was beside himself and didn't know what to do. His whole world was tumbling down around him.

Ed was quick to the rescue and told Greg to get his butt over to our office right away. Ed then told me his plan.

"I want to give Greg a cubicle here in our office," he said. "I want him to have free access to our phones, fax machine, and secretaries," he added. "I want him to feel like he belongs to something. I don't want him to be down in the dumps. I want him to come here in a suit and tie and feel like he's still part of the business world while he searches for his next job."

Ed's philosophy was that if Greg stayed home to look for a job, he would do everything but get a job. The house that has been waiting to be painted would get done, along with many other projects. Before long, a year would go by and Greg would still be looking for a job.

I readily agreed and a short time later Greg showed up. When we told Greg our plan, he was overwhelmed. His eyes teared up with gratitude and he couldn't thank us enough.

It took Greg a few months to land a new general manager position but when he did his rise was meteoric. In a few years he was the president of a group of radio stations, making big money, and now in a position to return the favor. We always stayed in touch until the time he passed away. He was one of the finest broadcasters and people I ever met. I know that Ed misses him a great deal also. What a loss.

146

Ed

Other times we helped our friends in the business by just giving advice. I would routinely help evaluate contracts for sales managers and general managers who were making a switch from one station to another, role-play with them before they went on interviews, and make calls on their behalf when they needed a recommendation.

In the movie *The Godfather*, Marlon Brandon's character, Don Vito Corleone, did favors for many people through out his life.

Whenever they asked, "What can I do for you, Godfather, to repay you for this great deed you have done for me?"

He would say, "Someday, I may call upon you to return this favor."

With us, we never had to ask. Everyone we helped (save one individual) couldn't wait to return the favor.

When we first started PriMedia we were looking for more companies to use our advertising agency's services. At that time a close friend of ours worked for a large prominent New England company and was promoted to VP/director of advertising. On his way up to that lofty position he had been dealing with his advertising agency and was very disappointed with its performance and personnel. He asked us if we would evaluate some of the work the agency had produced. After our evaluation we told him the things we would have done differently. He was very impressed, and he worked diligently to get us this piece of business. He succeeded, and we landed this prestigious account. We succeeded for him also as we quadrupled the sales of his product and won a prestigious ECHO Award (top award for direct response advertising) for our efforts. A few years later he decided to go out on his own and start a graphic design business. Of course, we were his first clients. Even now, years later, we still express our gratitude to this individual. He still does graphic design work for us. If we put a job out to bid and it is a tie, you know who wins all the ties, don't you?

That's the way it goes. He helped us, we helped him.

Sometimes helping others is a lot closer to home. Here's another story about a person who we hired, helped get ahead, and taught everything we could. He turned out to be one of the smartest business investments we ever made! This person came to work for us right out

147

of college. He had been a history/journalism major and wanted to get into the advertising business. He was a little wet behind the ears, but we hired him anyway as assistant to the creative director. He proved to be a quick learner and, when we terminated the employment of our creative director, he was in the position to take over. We told him that this was his chance to sink or swim, and he's been swimming laps around the pool ever since. He proved to be a true type A personality, which is unusual in a creative type of person. He was very aggressive and attacked each project we gave him with passion.

He was also the butt of one of our standard jokes, a take-off on a schtick from a popular film at the time (*My Favorite Year* with Peter O'Toole). He would come into the conference room with his idea of a new script and read it, and I would say, "Barry, do you smell something foul in here?"

Barry would reply, "WOW! That smell is awful."

I would say, "Do you know what it is?"

Barry would reply, "I don't know, but it seems to be coming from over there."

I would say, "Give me that script you just read." I would smell the script and say, "Yep, this is it! This script stinks!"

Barry

This person would grab the script and ask for specifics regarding what we liked and didn't like, and why. He would leave the room and soon come back with a different approach along the guidelines of what we had suggested. He understood the advertising phrase "there is no such thing as good writing, there is only good rewriting." As the years went by his ability to wear many hats impressed us. After we sold the company in 1984, he was one of only two people who we employed for a few years in our consulting business. The other was our longtime personal secretary. During those years we were fat cats who didn't want to work. We kept a small office, and this guy was relentless in trying to build the business. He would constantly be trying to get new consulting accounts for us. He would look for scriptwriting opportunities too, anything to bring a few dollars in the door and keep himself employed. If anything, we were an impediment to his aggressiveness. No matter how many hurdles we put in front of him by our casual attitude and general lack of interest, he managed to get us involved and working again.

Finally, when a new opportunity arose and we opened our current company, PriMedia, we were so appreciative of his prior efforts that we rewarded him with stock in the corporation, even though he knew virtually nothing about media buying, and we made him president/CEO. His aggressiveness continued and he managed to bring in a very large piece of business and manage many others.

While working for us at our previous company, he had fallen in love with one of the women in the bookkeeping department. A year later they were married. In fact, they cut their wedding cake with a Ginsu knife. Although a lot of companies have policies against married couples working for them, we didn't. We were thrilled for them. He quickly learned the ins and outs of our new business, and we realized that we were seeing him pick up our good habits while not picking up our bad ones. At times he was brilliant and at times he was a pain in the butt. If he wanted something done and we didn't like the idea, he would divide and conquer. He would get either one of us alone and re-pitch his idea. If he couldn't get one of us to agree he would go to the other one. If we still didn't agree, he would drop the subject for a few days and then start again: divide and conquer.

It would be improper to say he was ruthless, because he wasn't. But he was relentless. He refused to quit anything until he was shown in different ways why what he was proposing was not a good idea and he understood why—something we didn't always have the time, interest, or patience to provide. He just needed to be shown in different ways that what he was proposing was not a good idea. He really grew as a person and an executive over time. He took the company in new directions.

Ed

We had won numerous International ECHO Awards during our time in the direct response business. The ECHO Award is the highest award in the mail-order business. It is like getting an Oscar or an Emmy in direct marketing.

In fact, the tremendous success of our commercials and subsequent emergence of direct response television had caused the Direct Mail Marketing Association (DMMA) to change its name to the Direct Marketing Association (DMA).

The new direction that this employee took our company in was creating "brand direct" marketing campaigns for companies that combined elements of classic direct response and more conventional brand marketing in a way that had never been done before. This person constantly bounced his new ideas off us and the result was extremely successful campaigns for both New England Electric System company's compact fluorescent lightbulbs and Xerox's optical character recognition reader (named the Reading Edge) for the blind and visually impaired. Both campaigns succeeded way beyond expectations, and PriMedia received Gold ECHO awards for them even though they we up against the biggest advertising agencies in the world. Within a few short years the agency had been awarded more than 20 ECHO and New England Direct Marketing Association (NEDMA) awards for creative excellence and documented results for clients as diverse as the Massachusetts Highway Department and Air Canada.

As the years went by, he continued to impress us with his work ethic, honesty, and determination. His value to the company continued to increase and we offered him more stock in the company and even more responsibility. He accepted both and continued his work in the same fashion.

You see, the person I'm describing is actually James J. Cooney Jr., and our decision to "help" him by giving him the opportunity to work for and with us, and passing on as much of our combined knowledge as we could, has really helped us tremendously over the years in many, many ways.

He is honest, hardworking, aggressive, dedicated, and loyal. Jim's rapid and continual progress helped Barry comfortably reach a decision to retire a few years ago, and when he did so, Jim was able to purchase even more shares of PriMedia. At age 46, he has been president of the company for 14 years.

Helping others is a scenario that we were fortunate enough to be able to do many, many times over the years. From putting in a good word for somebody, to forwarding a resume, to offering some advice, a job, some business, or some temporary office space to work out of. Our initial investment of time, money, or energy has always seemed to pay off in a big way, whether it be additional business, personal satisfaction, or simply heartfelt gratitude.

We now have a treasure trove of people who are indebted to us or vice versa, and for that we are truly thankful. Some may repay our kindness and others may not. It doesn't really matter to us, because we have faith that things will work out as they are intended to. As far as we're concerned, it's a difficult world out there, so why not help each other out, as well as your self, at the same time. Win-win-win is the best situation of all.

Remember, "when you help others, you help yourself," so help as many people as you possibly can. You'll be amazed at how often your good deeds and good fortune are multiplied. They say "what goes around comes around" for a reason!

Hide Behind Rocks and Bushes

Ed

Ever watch movies about the British Colonial War? One thing that always struck me as odd were the so-called "British War Ethics." The British maintained such strict discipline and honor from their troops that it found its way on to the battlefield. They insisted that their troops march in a straight line when engaging their enemies. Plus, they expected that the enemy would honor their code of honor and not fire upon British officers. What were they thinking? Now, the Colonial armies and patriot soldiers who were fighting the British had a different philosophy. They said, "Okay, let me get this straight—you're going to march in a straight line while we hide behind rocks and bushes? How soon can we get started?"

Because this method was the way most armies in the world fought, the American patriot fighters separated themselves from the crowd by not doing what everyone else was doing at the time, and they went on to victory. This sort of "marching in a straight line" mentality was also employed by the English during their battles with Scottish clansmen, as seen in the movie *Braveheart*. Why would anyone fight a battle this way? At the time, those armies saw no reason to fight any other way. History has since given us many other answers to that question. Today, lots of people and companies act the way the British Army of the 17th and 18th centuries did. They continue to march in a straight line and never deviate simply because that's the way it's always been done. Why overthrow the status quo? Why rock the boat when you don't know how to swim? Why seek out new habitats, when you've always been a creature of habit? Simple. No stress. No thinking. Why tamper with tradition?

I am always amazed when I ask someone who is simply maintaining "status quo," someone who just "goes along to get along," someone who marches in a straight line and wouldn't even consider doing it any other way, "So, how is business?"

I usually get, "Actually, business is good," or "My career is moving along just fine."

I love it when I get a chance to say, "Compared to what?" As long as that person is doing well, he or she is content. However, ask yourself, what could your business be doing or where could your career be if you didn't always follow the crowd? What if you break tradition and try something new? These are questions that you will never know the answers to unless you try. There is simply no other way that I know of. Some people call it "risk-taking" and find it incredibly frightening. I say, if it involves believing in yourself, it's more like "calculated risk-*making*," and it's incredibly exhilarating! If you're not going to be confident about your own capabilities and bet on yourself to succeed, I'm going to bet that you're *destined* to be a failure. It's a self-fulfilling prophecy that you can shape and mold a different way if you simply believe it can be done. If you can see it, you can be it. That's where it all begins.

Barry

When you were in elementary school, every few months you would get a report card and you would find out how well or poorly you were doing in various subjects. It's too bad it doesn't work that way in the business world. Out there in the "real world" you find out how you're doing at your job at your annual review. If you find out sooner, it's usually not good news. What really amazes me is that the elementary school model hasn't made it into the business world.

During my 40 years of being in business for myself I have never had an employee come to me and say, "Boss, how am I doing? What can I improve on? How can I make myself more valuable to you and the company?" Or this one, "I don't have enough work to keep me busy all day long. Any chance I can do more?" Yeah, that'll happen!

Boy, would I be impressed with an employee who hit me with those questions! My opinion of that person would go up a few thousand percent. Just think, you can be the only person in your company who cares enough to ask how you can help more. It would surely separate you from the crowd.

Ed

When I was in the military (National Guard) we would have a weekend drill each month. Now, I don't want you to think that the National Guard isn't a ready organization, because it is indeed ready and able to step in and help, not only in overseas theatres such as the Middle East, but here at home as well. But, for the most part, these drills consisted of what we would call "make work details." I was attached to an artillery battalion, so my company would clean Howitzers (big guns) most of the weekends. Despite the fact that we had cleaned them last month and they hadn't moved, we would clean them again. The amazing thing was that no one seemed to mind.

One day, a lowly private went up to the first sergeant and said, "Sarge, this is bull!@#$! I am doing nothing constructive. Isn't there something else I can do?"

The sergeant said, "Yes there is. What do you do for a living?"

The private proceeded to tell the sergeant that he had a job as an accountant at a big firm in the city.

The sergeant said, "We are backed up on clerical work. Come with me." Every drill we attended from that point on, this private worked with the company clerks. Soon the private became a corporal, and then a sergeant and the new company clerk. At first we thought, "What a kiss ass." We changed our minds quickly as he increased his rank and his pay. He had won the respect of the first sergeant and the company officers.

Barry

Everything we did in our careers separated us from the crowd. We marched to the tune of a different drummer. Madison Avenue produced 30-second commercials; we did two-minute commercials. No one took TV orders by credit card because there was no system; we created a system. We sold knives with two competing knife of-fers on the air, when the last thing on anyone's mind was, "I need more knives." Throughout this book there are many examples of how we did things differently. It is the essence of our success. I can honestly say that if we did not break the rules, we would not have been as successful as we are today. We would have followed the crowd by doing the traditional, and marched right off the cliff over and over again.

Perhaps the only thing that differentiates you from the person sitting next to you is your willingness to take the first step off the beaten path toward cover, while everyone else continues to march in a straight line.

People are counting on you, and there is a lot at stake! You can-not afford to wait for things to happen. You must make your own luck. That starts when you stop marching in a straight line and start "hiding behind rocks and bushes." All's fair in love and war; and make no mistake about it, running a successful business or having a suc-cessful career is the longest war you'll ever engage in!

Check Your Check

Ed

One of the reasons why Barry and I were successful together is that we constantly played off one another. My weakness would be Barry's strength, and vice versa. Our character traits were also interchangeable. For example, Barry has this habit of constantly looking over the bill in a restaurant for mistakes. What's incredible is that he finds something about 30 percent of the time. If six people were dining, there should only be six meals on the check. Then, to finish, Barry checks the math. Now I don't want to disparage waitresses or waiters, because they work very hard for their money and put up with a lot, but, like all of us, they are human and are subject to making mistakes. One night in New York City, Barry found a $120 mistake.

157

The Wisdom of Ginsu

Obviously, this practice was immediately incorporated into my behavior. "Great idea," you might be saying to yourself, right? Yes, but the lesson here goes much further. The objective is not to just teach you to check your restaurant checks, but to check all the checks and whomever is writing them. After all, people are people: some are honest, some are not; some are smart, some are not. But all of them make mistakes. During our careers somehow we got to meet all of these people. Life would sure be wonderful if everyone was honest and had a lot of integrity and everyone never made a mistake. Alas, this is not Mayberry RFD, and life is such that we have to watch our backs in business as well as in our personal lives. Hey! If we don't do it, who will? Unfortunately, we learned this Ginsuism the hard way. Here are a couple of examples.

We were rolling right along, getting rich selling Ginsu, Armourcote cookware, Lustreware, and DuraSteel mixing bowls. It never occurred to us at the time that we should be watching our back. One day while Barry was visiting his dentist for a check-up, he told Barry while sitting in the chair, "My son bought my wife a whole bunch of your products for her birthday. She got the pots and pans, the knives, the bowls, everything!" When the dental probe was removed from Barry's mouth, he asked, "Did he come to the office for them? I would have given him a discount if I knew they were for you." He replied, "No, he got them at your discount place downtown. He paid half price." Barry almost needed oxygen. We didn't have a discount place downtown. Alarm bells were now going off his head.

Barry

As soon as I was finished with the dentist I headed back to the office and called an emergency meeting. It was obvious that our inventory was walking itself out of our warehouse and was being sold downtown. Evidently, we had a partner or two we didn't know about. Now, when most people were hired they submitted a resume and we checked them out thoroughly, but the warehouse help were usually high school dropouts. They were young and inexperienced and had no work record to check, and we paid them minimum wage. We were seeking brawn, not brains.

158

Check Your Check

We were really good at selling products on the television, but as inventory-control managers we stunk. Instead of reporting it to the police, we decided that we would investigate the situation ourselves. After a week or so we were no closer to catching the culprit, so we decided that the smartest thing we could do was hire an undercover investigator. Where do you go to hire an undercover investigator? How about a detective agency? We called one and they sent over a so-called detective. He looked like he was 16 years old. They told us he would fit right in because of his youthful appearance. They also told us that we had to put him on our payroll as an employee plus we had to pay them a substantial fee on top of his salary. We were determined to find the thief, so we acquiesced.

He was supposed to make friends with the warehouse crew and go out with them for a few beers and try to get in on the action. After the first week he reported to us that he had nothing to tell us. The second week his report was the same as the first one. After the third week passed and his report was identical to the others we began to wonder if it wouldn't be less expensive to let the stealing continue. Sometime during the fourth week his report to us changed. Now, you are thinking that he came to us with news of his discovery of the thief's identity. Not quite! He reported that he was leaving the detective agency for a job somewhere else. We were more than mildly upset. What we had was four more lost weeks with more merchandise undoubtedly going out the door, and a wasted effort with the detective agency. We told the agency what they could do with their bill and decided to attack the situation ourselves.

We interviewed separately everyone who came into contact with our merchandise in the warehouse. The only person we considered above suspicion was the warehouse manager. We had originally hired him for a menial position but he showed so much intelligence, charm, and energy that he was rapidly promoted to customer service manager and then to warehouse manager. We gave him that position because of our implicit trust in him. Our detective technique was to tell each person that we knew who the thief was and ask him if he was also involved.

Each and every one of them professed their innocence. They did it in such a way that we thought that they were telling the truth. We were puzzled. The merchandise definitely had legs. It was sure walking out of the building. We decided to interview the warehouse manager. When we told him we knew who was doing the stealing, his confession startled us. We couldn't believe it. We had such high hopes for this person. He explained that he felt he was demoted when he went from customer service manager to warehouse manager, because as customer service manager he had eight people working for him and now he had only three. We were shocked. Apparently the raise we had given him meant nothing to him. The additional responsibility given him as guardian of the Ginsu hadn't registered. When we asked him how he did it, he said, "It was simple. You gave me complete control over the inventory, and you never bothered to check."

He offered to pay us back for what had gone missing and begged for his job back. We said that we would take the money in exchange for not reporting him to the police, but his job was history and not to expect any references from us. Last we heard, instead of being an advertising executive, which he would have been had he stayed with us, he was bartending in California. Not that there's anything wrong with tending bar, but we are sure he's making about $200,000 a year less than he'd be making if he kept his hands clean and stayed with us.

We didn't check the check or check the checker!

In Las Vegas, the casino operations do a great job of checking. The casino manager watches the shift manager, who watches the pit bosses, who watch the floorman, who watches the boxman, who watches the dealers (with the eye-in-the-sky cameras in the ceiling) watching everybody. This is an extreme example, but when that kind of money is involved, it's necessary.

Talk to an owner of a small restaurant and you'll find that he is always there on site. Why? Because money is exchanged the entire time the restaurant is open. Temptation mixed with opportunity. People are people, and that is why you'll find many references in this book about taking control of your business and career by getting more involved in how things run. Never overlook even the smallest detail, as it can mushroom out of control.

Check Your Check

Ed

Some of our very close friends own a number of very successful small businesses. You know you're a "very successful" small business owner when you suddenly realize that you've gone from doing and knowing everything about your business on a daily basis to getting the occasional very strong feeling, more and more often, that you know very little about too many things regarding your business. You begin to forget to "check your check," or you don't have time to "check your check." It's understandable. This is what you work so hard for every day, isn't it? So you can have extra time and money to do the things you want?

Well that's exactly what happened to one of our friends: he wasn't "checking his check." Fifteen years ago he stopped checking his checks by trusting a particular employee with more and more financial responsibility without a double-check system in place. He checked his bank statements occasionally, and they always balanced, because he never dreamed anything was wrong and he never imagined that his trusted employee was steaming open the envelopes and removing the fraudulent checks she was writing to embezzle from him for years and years. When finally caught (she came forward as the result of an unexpected internal audit in conjunction with the company's accounting firm) do you know how much she had stolen over 15 years? More than $500,000. What's even worse is that she spent every penny of the money on gambling and had no assets left to go after.

Check your check: it can add up to a lot of money, especially with interest, and it happens every day to thousands of businesses nationwide!

Take stock of the people you work for and the people you work with. Don't assume that everything is okay; check to be sure. People make mistakes, people commit crimes, and people are not perfect. Any piece of paper with a number on it can be wrong intentionally or otherwise, so you need to check everyone whenever and however you can. Sure some people are going to think that you're a pain in the butt, but do you really care?

Every state in the country has a local business paper or business section of the daily paper that's full of weekly listings of bankrupt small businesses that might still be around today if they had only "checked their check" to make sure it was correct, whether that means daily financial records and reports, bank statements, office supplies, expense accounts, or mileage reimbursements. Even when it comes to the work your employees are submitting to your customers or the supervisors you have working for you, you should never assume that everything is fine. In fact, you owe it to yourself, your company, and your customers to make sure it is right, even if it means having your partner or an outside source double-check your check!

Even if you have everything it takes to be successful and do what we did, it can all come unraveled in the blink of an eye if you forget to "check your check." What kind of people do you have working for you? How sure are you? How accurate are the figures you're basing daily decisions on? Are you being charged the correct amount? Are you double-checking your accounts payable invoices and statements to be sure? Are you paying too fast and needlessly affecting your cash flow? Too slow and hurting your credit rating?

Remember to "check your check" every single day. The decision and the price you ultimately pay—higher or lower—is literally in your hands each and every day!

You Never Know From Where the Cash Is Gonna Flow

EASY TO CLEAN

Barry

In sports we have all heard from our coaches to keep our eye on the ball. But you really have to keep your eyes open and on the ball off the field as well. So much information is thrown at us on a daily basis. The competition for your "eyeballs" is very fierce. It not only comes at us visually, but also verbally. Cars rush by us as we travel to work. People are constantly passing us in the streets and in the malls. We tend to take all this aural and visual input for granted. It becomes the visual and aural garbage of daily life. But how much are we really missing? How many opportunities are we missing? Are we missing key visual signals from our superiors at work? From our families and loved ones? Do we have selective attention? Do we let the din of voices around us crowd out important statements? Is the glare of visual input stopping us from seeing where our next dollar is coming from? Ed always makes sure the answers to these questions are no, no, and no! And you should too!

In today's fast-paced world there are many opportunities that just fly by us in the left lane at 100 MPH. There are signposts up ahead, and your job is to read them before your next move. How? One way is to slow down and train your mind to look at everything as a possible opportunity to succeed and make money. We all dismiss many opportunities because we are so busy, but the trick here is to dismiss them selectively, not arbitrarily. One of the many lessons this business has taught me is that you look at every bit of information being thrown at you as an opportunity. Yes, everything has promise until I find a reason for it not to. I can tell you that if someone had said to me that I would be writing a book today about the lessons I learned from selling gadgets on TV, I would have said he was crazy. I also could have easily dismissed that idea as crazy. Think about it. It does sound crazy. Here's a great example of what I am talking about.

In 1980, after we had completed our buyout of the Englishmen, our Lustreware flatware product had steadily climbed to sales of 20,000 sets a week. We were originally buying the flatware product from a local company in Rhode Island that was buying the flatware from a manufacturer in Korea and marking the price up 10 percent and selling it to us. That company was sure happy with the deal. We had to give them a letter of guarantee that, upon the merchandise entering the country, they would be paid. All this middleman was doing was piggybacking the letter of credit to the manufacturer in Korea. There was absolutely no risk involved but the reward was excessive. For handling the paperwork they were making $18,000 a week. Not a bad deal at all. With the buyout ongoing, we were too busy to give the situation the time it deserved, but when it was completed we attacked it. We met with the middleman and told him we wanted a reduction in the fee and at the same time we contacted various custom brokers and import firms in an attempt to purchase the product directly from a manufacturer. The middleman was adamant in his refusal to reduce his price even by 1 cent. The handwriting was on the wall for him. We had to find a better way.

Ed

Through our efforts we received a call one day from a fellow we'll call Charles. Barry took Charles's call and listened to the pitch. Charles was promising the world. He said he would get the same exact flatware from the same manufacturer and sell it to us for the same $9 price the middleman was paying. He said he would take us on a tour of the Orient, all expenses paid, to look for new products. Best of all, he said his fee would be paid by the manufacturer in Korea and wouldn't affect the price we paid.

Now, Barry had heard a lot of sales pitches in his time, but somehow this guy Charles seemed sincere and Barry felt that having a meeting with Charles couldn't hurt. A meeting occurred shortly thereafter and Charles explained that he constantly traveled through the Orient, buying and selling products and looking for new items to sell in the States. He claimed to know many manufactures in the Orient and, best of all, he said he knew the maker of our Lustreware product very well and he would bring the Korean manufacturer to our office in Rhode Island for a clandestine meeting. The reason for the secrecy was because the Korean company was now selling the 20,000 sets a week of Lustreware to our middleman and didn't want to jeopardize that business, even if we were the final buyer.

Sure enough, 10 days later Charles appeared at our office one evening with two Korean gentlemen. One was the owner of the factory and the other was his translator and right-hand man for American business. After much discussion in which we explained that we were going to find another flatware maker if he didn't sell directly to us at $9 and that he would lose the current business that we had with our middleman, he acquiesced and also agreed that Charles's compensation would be his responsibility.

Charles had done it. He had delivered on his promise. Our letters of credit now went directly to Korea and we were saving $18,000 a week. Charles then insisted upon delivering on his other promise.

The Wisdom of Ginsu

He practically demanded that we accompany him on a product-finding trip to the Orient. Now, Charles was quite a smoothie—or so he thought. He carefully explained that it was a 17-hour flight to Korea from New England. He would fly us first class to Seattle and then we would meet him in Seattle and fly together in coach to Seoul. He further explained that coach was a much better way to travel to the Orient because each one of us could sleep across three seats laying down rather than being uncomfortable in a single somewhat reclining first-class seat. We figured he was a little light on cash so we said, "Sure, we'll do it." He was sure right about the sleeping quarters as we all got a good eight hours sleep in the back of the 747.

Barry

We were met by a limo and driver and taken to a beautiful high-rise hotel in downtown Seoul. On the way to our hotel we passed by many tanks armed with machine guns. The driver explained that there had been some unrest recently and that there was a curfew in effect. Everyone had to be off the street by 10 p.m. or they could be shot. At that point we told the driver to turn around and take us back to the airport because we wanted to "get the heck out of Dodge." The driver had no idea what a "Dodge" was, or why the hell we would want to get out of it, but assured us that no one had been shot (yet!) and that he would have us to our hotel by 9:30 p.m. at the latest. We felt a little better about things until we pulled up in front of the hotel, which was in a tall skyscraper in downtown Seoul. Right in front of the hotel's entrance was a tank with a machine gunner perched on top of it. It seemed that everyone was ignoring the fact that a machine gunner was staring at them, so we decided to stick it out. After a good dinner and trying again without success to sleep, it was clear that the 12-hour time difference was getting to us. Sleep was impossible, so after staying up all night and having a good breakfast, we headed off to the Lustreware factory.

It was on this factory tour that a few amazing things happened. When we toured the factory we were amazed that when ever an employee passed by the owner they stopped and bowed.

166

You Never Know From Where the Cash Is Gonna Flow

We thought this was a wonderful practice and we were anxious to bring the bowing custom back to the States with us. The only trouble was that all our employees probably would have quit rather than be an early adopter of the bow.

Then when we asked for a bathroom, we were amazed to discover that there were no urinals or toilets. The only things available were holes in the ground. This was definitely an invention that we had never seen before (and one that we could do without).

After touring this large factory, we entered the showroom. Stainless steel pieces were everywhere and a lot of them didn't look particularly stainless. They certainly weren't dust-free. After looking around for a while we were about to leave when Ed bent down and retrieved something from under a table. He motioned me over and said, "This is our next product."

Being the domestically challenged person that I am, I looked at what Ed was holding as asked, "What is it?"

Ed looked back at me and said, "I'll tell you later."

That evening, after dinner, I once again asked Ed what he had picked up. Ed explained that it was a mixing bowl made of stainless steel and that they were going to sell a ton of them. It turned out that this was a serious understatement (more about that a little later).

Ed

The next morning we went to the Taiwan Embassy and received visas for a two-day stay and boarded a plane for that island. I found Taiwan exciting. The airport was new and gleaming of stainless steel and modern in every way. Not at all what I expected. I don't know why, but I expected an airport that was in need of repair with the long rolling stairways leading out of the plane onto the tarmac and into the airport. What we got were jetways that rival any airport I have ever been in. During a spectacular authentic Chinese lunch, we all laughed at Barry, who asked the waiter for a fork. To this day, I have never been able to find Chinese food that great, as I always make the comparison to Taiwan. After lunch we visited many factories, stocked up on samples and business cards, and then returned to the hotel for a quiet dinner and then some well-deserved sleep. It was mildly curious that in looking over the many business cards that I collected through-out the day that all of my contacts had Chinese last names with American first names: names such as Bill Chang or Bobby Lee.

From Taiwan it was off to Hong Kong. After an uneventful flight we checked into the Hong Kong Sheraton Hotel. The Hong Kong Sheraton is located in the popular Tsimshatsui area and overlooks Victoria Harbor and Hong Kong Island. One of the features of this hotel is a rooftop pool that offers an impressive view of Hong Kong. Because we were suffering from jet lag, we decided to take the day off and get some sun.

Upon arriving at the pool and looking at the wonderful scenery around Hong Kong, we retired to the custom-made lounges around the pool and noticed that many of the other people around us had a little black box in their hands with a wire running up to their ears. There were little soft pads on their ears. We had no idea what these were all about. The people were also moving their lips and some were tapping their fingers. We discussed the situation and decided that these devices must be some type of physical therapy machine that sent an electrical pulse to the fingers, lips, and ears. It was the only thing that made sense. We decided to ask someone what the device was. The reply was in a foreign language that we didn't understand. We asked someone else; the reply was equally indistinguishable. A third person shooed us away. After taking a swim and getting some sun, the person next to us detached himself from this black box and jumped in the pool. Now, with our curiosity piqued to the heavens, we decided to investigate.

Stealing a peek at the black box we discovered the name Sony stamped on it. But what did it do? We still didn't know. That evening when we met Charles for dinner we were treated to a wonderful dinner featuring shark fin soup and other Chinese delicacies.

Later we asked him if he knew what this strange lip-moving, finger-tapping device was. Charles didn't have any idea and only wanted to talk about our upcoming visit to a cookware factory. It wasn't until two years later when Sony introduced the Walkman that we found out what the product was.

Barry

To this day, new Japanese electronic products are available in Japan a couple of years before arriving in America. Recently I was at a wedding in San Diego and I was using my new Sony TR notebook computer. I was telling a friend that it only weighed 3.1 pounds when another friend said that his new Sharp computer only weighed 2.5 pounds and had all the same features as my Sony. I am a person who keeps abreast of the tech world's developments, but I was shocked that I hadn't yet heard of this new computer. My friend told me that he had just been to Japan and had spotted the computer and purchased it immediately. He further explained that he was told that his new computer might never be sold in the United States.

Ed

Hong Kong is truly a city of mystery and intrigue. When we were there it felt like we were in the middle of a James Bond film surrounded by international businessmen and other "movers and shakers" from all over the world in their tailored three-piece suits and tuxedos. There were exotic-looking characters, and even more exotic-looking shops, merchandise, food, and vehicles everywhere. The streets were bustling with activity even at 2 or 3 in the morning. In fact, when we returned to our hotel from a late dinner and meeting, we saw many couples in the lobby sharply dressed and just beginning to go out on the town. Hong Kong is a shopper's paradise, with store after store of just about anything and everything you could possibly want at incredibly reasonable prices.

From an adman's perspective I couldn't help but marvel at the one-upmanship the store owner's exhibited with their signage. Each shop and store owner for block after block was obviously trying to outdo the other with bigger, taller, and longer signs that extended out from their buildings over the sidewalks and beyond, forming virtual signage tunnels that dominated your view for blocks and blocks on end. Someone explained that in the beginning when someone put out a sign, the neighboring shop would put its up higher and wider, so as to be seen better and grab more attention. This practice snowballed until the storeowners and signs had (literally) gone as far as they could go.

Another thing I noticed about Hong Kong was the incredible number of small companies on the island. Most seemed to consist of a family living in a second- or third-floor apartment, where they made their product, while eating and sleeping in adjoining rooms. In many cases it appeared that the entire family, including children, was working for the company. If you responded to a full-page ad in an import/export catalog and had been corresponding with, for example, the Hong Kong Widget Company from your office in the United States, you would be impressed and would probably picture a large manufacturing facility with modern offices and a large number of employees. However, if you actually travel to Hong Kong, you are just as likely to discover that the Hong Kong Widget Company is really one of these small family firms being run out of a two-bedroom apartment!

Barry

When we awoke the next morning and headed out to breakfast we were accosted by a clothing salesman in the mall that was attached to the hotel asking us if we were interested in a custom-made suit. Ed explained that we had to catch a plane to the States at noon and, because it was 8 a.m., he didn't have time to buy a suit.

The salesman said, " No problem."

He promised that he would have the suits done before we left and that he would deliver the suits to us at the airport. Now how could anyone turn down an offer like that? I explained that I didn't want a suit, but that I would take a beautiful leather jacket like the one in the window. We negotiated a price of $100 for the suit and $70 for the leather jacket. We negotiated everything. The salesman led us into the shop and showed us numerous pieces of leather for the jacket and rolls and rolls of material for Ed's suit. After we had picked out the material we were both measured everywhere: legs, wrists, back, chest, and so on. He said that we should go have breakfast and come back in an hour for another fitting. At breakfast we laughed at the impossibility of having the clothing done in the next few hours. Then we headed back to the store to see if anything was happening. Lo and behold, he had the suit and jacket partially sewn together and proceeded to do more measuring and adjustments. We were told to come back at 11 a.m. for a final fitting. At 11 a.m. we arrived with carry-on baggage in hand and were once more adjusted and fitted. It still did not look possible for the stuff to be done in an hour. Then we headed for the airport. We kept looking at our watches as boarding time neared. Then out of nowhere as we were just about to board the aircraft the salesman came running through the airport and grabbed us before we could board. He handed us each a box and asked for his money. We paid him and were amazed. We couldn't believe he had done it.

On the way home I turned to Ed and said, "What if the suit and jacket aren't in the boxes?"

Ed replied, "Son-of-a-gun, we've probably been conned."

First thing we did when we arrived back home was to open the boxes. Sure enough, the clothing was there. I put on the leather jacket and it fit perfectly. Ed tried on his suit and it was better than he expected. We were thoroughly impressed.

Upon finishing our business in Hong Kong we were informed by Charles that he would not be returning to the States with us. He had additional business in Hong Kong and would be staying there. Ed immediately picked up the phone and called Pan Am for an upgrade to first class. For $600 each we would get to taste the first class cabin on the 18-hour trip back home on the 747. Charles took us to the terminal and insisted on going inside with us where there were about 300 passengers in line at the coach boarding area, so we went to the first class line. Charles said, "You can't go there! That's for first class only."

I said, "Because you're not going with us, we decided to upgrade."

Charles stammered, "Y-y-you w-won't have much sleeping room," and he left the airport. The flight from Hong Kong to San Francisco took 11 and 1/2 hours and we were served the finest wines, caviar, and even had the opportunity to cut our own piece of prime rib from the rib cart. Bread was served in a basket made out of twisted bread and the booze was unlimited. The bathrooms had toothbrushes and cologne, and everyone received slippers and toothpaste. But we had to admit that Charles was right about one thing: it was sure better sleeping across three seats in coach than one seat in first class.

Upon arriving back in Rhode Island we were anxious to receive the sample products we had ordered while in the Orient. Ed was particularly anxious to get his hands on some of those mixing bowls he had found under the table in Korea. He already had a plan for them. When we arrived back at the office the creative meetings started. Research was done by going to major department stores and seeing what the competition was. No one was selling stainless steel mixing bowls. Tupperware was the dominant party in the mixing bowl area, doing, as I read, more than a billion dollars a year, and the only product in stores were Tupperware knock-offs. The prospect of this product being successful was becoming evident. The only thing we needed was a good zig. As the offer took shape we decided that we would sell a 1-quart, 2-quart, 3-quart, 5-quart, and a gigantic 8-quart mixing bowl. These bowls could easily nest inside each other and take up very little storage space.

Now we needed a "but wait, there's more."

We decided to add chrome utensils, which included an extra-large spoon, ladle, fork, whisk, and spaghetti server, but we still felt that wasn't enough. I brought up the point that the bowls would have to be covered in order to store food, so we decided to prevail upon the manufacturer to create plastic covers that would tightly fit each bowl. While showing all five bowls we would use the line, "What could possibly top this? Covers!" and the covers would virtually pop onto each of the bowls.

Now we needed one of our crazy openings. We felt that we had to knock Tupperware if we were going to be successful. We had to show the positive side of stainless steel bowls and the negative side of plastic and glass bowls. How would you do that? We worked on it for a while and did some tests. Sure enough, putting tuna fish in a plastic bowl gave the bowl a lasting odor, and putting a blowtorch to it melted it instantly. The odor of the tuna fish washed right out of the stainless steel bowls, and the blowtorch didn't even mar it. Dropping a glass bowl shattered it into pieces; dropping a stainless steel bowl didn't even dent it. Somehow we had to come up with an opening that graphically showed fish odor. The one we came up with was, "We are going to give this plastic bowl something that will last forever...fish odor. It can turn your birthday cake into a fish cake." The video showed a birthday cake with a fish through it. Then we went on to demonstrate the bowls. Last but hardly least we had to agree on a selling price and a name for the product.

Fish cake.

The name we came up with was Royal DuraSteel mixing bowls. This gave the impression that the bowls were fit for royalty and made of durable steel. The selling price would be $29.95.

Royal DuraSteel.

Now that the front-end work was done it was time to test the product, so we put it on eight television stations. The public bought it

173

rapidly, so we added 10 more stations. Orders came in like crazy, and 40 more stations brought the same results. We had another winner! We expanded it nationwide and the orders kept on coming, and the cost of advertising per order (CPO) kept dropping. Orders magically climbed to almost 20,000 per week for a weekly cash intake on Royal DuraSteel of $600,000. It was a shame, but Royal DuraSteel was one of the shortest-running products in our career. You see, once the commercials started running nationwide buyers from large department store chains started buying large quantities of nested stainless steel mixing bowls and our product's future was doomed. Once mixing bowls were available in every mall, no one would send a check and wait 30 days to receive their mixing bowls when they could get them now at a store up the road. Nevertheless, Royal DuraSteel mixing bowls sold more than 600,000 units, totaling $18 million in sales, in the one year it was running on television. Not bad for a product that was found under a table by an alert Ed Valenti.

Remember, "you never know from where your cash is gonna to flow," so keep your eyes and mind open to the many possibilities of future income.

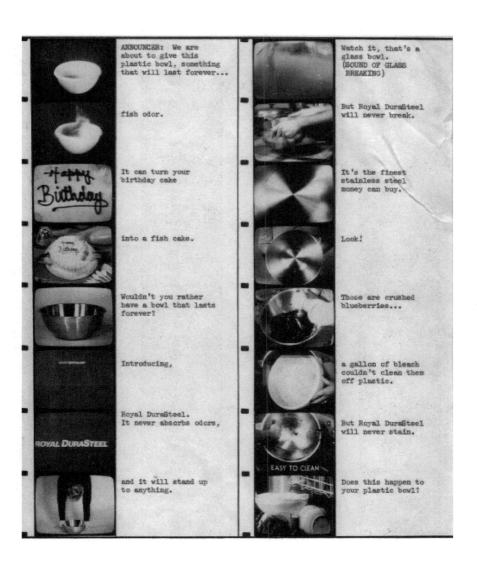

ANNOUNCER: We are
about to give this
plastic bowl, something
that will last forever...

fish odor.

It can turn your
birthday cake

into a fish cake.

Wouldn't you rather
have a bowl that lasts
forever?

Introducing,

Royal DuraSteel.
It never absorbs odors,

and it will stand up
to anything.

Watch it, that's a
glass bowl.
(SOUND OF GLASS
BREAKING)

But Royal DuraSteel
will never break.

It's the finest
stainless steel
money can buy.

Look!

These are crushed
blueberries...

a gallon of bleach
couldn't clean them
off plastic.

But Royal DuraSteel
will never stain.

Does this happen to
your plastic bowl?

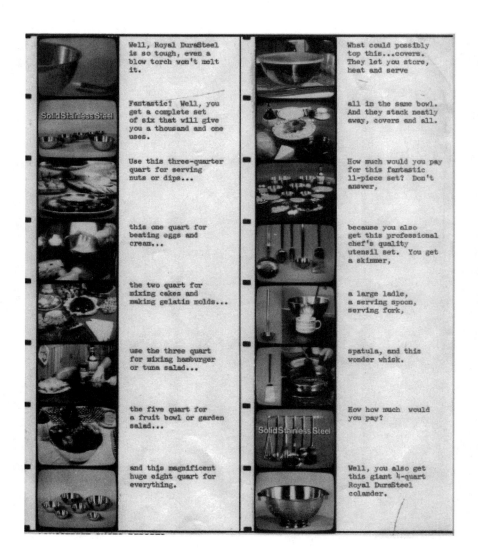

Well, Royal DuraSteel is so tough, even a blow torch won't melt it.

Fantastic? Well, you get a complete set of six that will give you a thousand and one uses.

Use this three-quarter quart for serving nuts or dips...

this one quart for beating eggs and cream...

the two quart for mixing cakes and making gelatin molds...

use the three quart for mixing hamburger or tuna salad...

the five quart for a fruit bowl or garden salad...

and this magnificent huge eight quart for everything.

What could possibly top this...covers. They let you store, heat and serve

all in the same bowl. And they stack neatly away, covers and all.

How much would you pay for this fantastic 11-piece set? Don't answer,

because you also get this professional chef's quality utensil set. You get a skimmer,

a large ladle, a serving spoon, serving fork,

spatula, and this wonder whisk.

How how much would you pay?

Well, you also get this giant 4-quart Royal DuraSteel colander.

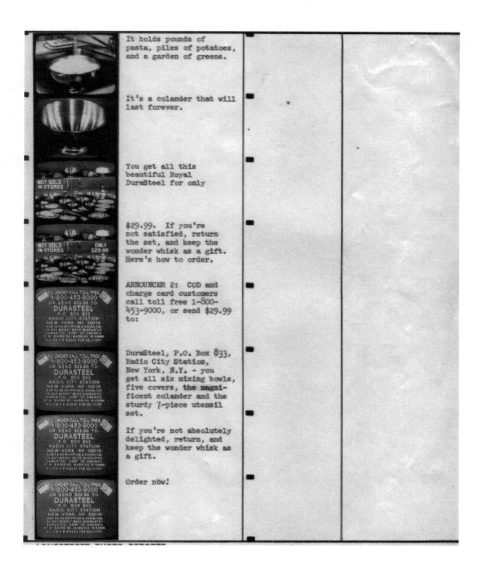

It holds pounds of pasta, piles of potatoes, and a garden of greens.

It's a colander that will last forever.

You get all this beautiful Royal DuraSteel for only

$29.99. If you're not satisfied, return the set, and keep the wonder whisk as a gift. Here's how to order.

ANNOUNCER 2: COD and charge card customers call toll free 1-800-453-9000, or send $29.99 to:

DuraSteel, P.O. Box 833, Radio City Station, New York, N.Y. - you get all six mixing bowls, five covers, the magnificent colander and the sturdy 7-piece utensil set.

If you're not absolutely delighted, return, and keep the wonder whisk as a gift.

Order now!

LARGE DOUBLE BOILER

BABY FOOD WARMER

20

Start at the Top

Ed

I often wonder how we all became so accustomed to starting at the bottom. Perhaps it's fear or perhaps it's military training and the chain of command. You know, ask the corporal first, then he goes to the sergeant, and on and on. I guess it doesn't really matter how we learned this behavior, because this chapter is about starting at the top. I remember reading a story in a magazine about a successful business executive who credited his success to emulating the successful people he met in his life. Whatever they did, he did. He went on to say, "The road map is here for all to see." One of the tactics he employed was only starting at the top in every business encounter. He learned it from a former boss, now he does it always. Getting the message here?

Now, I don't want you to think that starting at the top is always easy and works every time, because it does not. However, if you believe in numbers, the law of averages is on your side. In other words, it works enough of the time to make the effort worthwhile. I have found over and over again that if you truly want something done, if you really want action, you have to start at the top. That's where the decision-makers live.

Now let's explore what happens if you are not successful and all of your attempts are blocked. Sometimes what you end up with is dealing or speaking with individuals who are several management layers lower, but you come with an introduction from the top. That can be as good as dealing at the top directly.

It is interesting that most lower-level employees seem to feel that they are protecting their company when they make a customer service decision that, in the long term, is not in the best interests of their company. When you go to return something and a bored clerk says, "We can't take that back, it's company policy," is that really serving the company's best interest?

Whenever I hear the words "It's company policy," I ask to speak to the manager. It is worth a few minutes of time even though the manager is only on top at the local branch. If that doesn't work, it is time to go to the real top, the president of the company.

Let's take the situation Barry had with a major moving company when he retired to Florida a few years ago. When the moving van arrived at his new home and the massive truck doors were opened, many pieces of his furniture went flying out of the truck onto the ground. Needless to say, there was extensive damage to these pieces. You see, the movers had jammed the furniture into a space that was much too small to hold it. After all the furniture was unloaded and moved into the house, Barry asked the driver for the procedure to file a claim. The driver outlined the procedure and Barry quickly filed a claim for the damages. About two weeks later he received a letter denying his claim because the procedure he used was the wrong one. Barry then wrote a certified letter to the president of the company.

Within 48 hours he received a call from an adjuster who wanted to look at the damaged furniture. Two weeks later he received a check for more than $2,000 covering the claim. Barry's new neighbors mentioned that when they moved in they had the same type of damage problem with a different moving company. They also said that they had been waiting almost a year for the situation to be resolved. Maybe if they started at the top, the result would have been different.

Throughout my entire career, I always try to talk with the people who can make the decisions. The people at the top or the decision-makers are more accessible than you would think. Try! Ask! When I have a problem with anything I always ask, "Would you please direct me to the person who is in a position to make a decision about this?" Earlier in my career when I sold vacuum cleaners door to door, I never demonstrated one to just the housewife. Why? Because she would always say, "My husband is the boss; he makes the decisions." Even if it wasn't true, she said it anyway, just to get rid of me. I became more successful and sold more vacuums in less time by simply showing it only to both husband and wife together. Always make a concerted effort to reach and speak with the decision-maker. Because most don't, you'll be ahead of the crowd.

Barry

Back in 1982 when we decided to introduce our second set of nonstick pots and pans, which we promptly dubbed Armourcote II, we had many issues to discuss with the manufacturer Mirro Aluminum.

First on the list was product selection, so we hired a small jet and flew to Manitowoc, Wisconsin, the home of Mirro. During the review of just about everything Mirro made we were regrettably told that is was virtually impossible to sell nonstick bakeware with nonstick cookware. They told us that it had been tried many times and had always been unsuccessful. So, of course, because experience is the best teacher, we first picked out all the nonstick cookware we thought would make up a good offer and had it shipped to Rhode Island.

The Wisdom of Ginsu

After spending a few weeks with the samples selected we still felt that the offer wasn't strong enough, so we called Mirro and had them ship us many nonstick bakeware pieces. Once more representatives from Mirro told us that it would be foolish to merge the bakeware and the cookware in the same offer. Too stubborn to realize that it couldn't be done, we set out to make a commercial selling both cookware and bakeware.

Could we prove the experts wrong? We decided to open the commercial with a chicken being dropped on a diamond ring on a woman's hand. How on earth could this sell a $30 cookware set? We would use the line, "A diamond is the hardest surface known to man, but two years later you still can't cook on it! That's why you need Armourcote II with bigger and better pieces."

During the editing of the commercial one of editors saw the footage of this chicken dropping on the woman's hand and screamed out, "Oh my God! What are they doing now?"

He couldn't believe that we would open a commercial with an ugly raw chicken. The commercial then proceeded to sell an assortment of nonstick pots and pans and even a 5-quart Dutch oven. How much would you pay for all these pots and pans? Don't answer, because we'll give you even more. *But wait, there's more!* You'll even get nonstick bakeware. Now how much would you pay? Once the product selection was complete, it was time to start at the top.

Apparently Mirro felt the same way. I agreed to meet the president of Mirro at the Hilton at Boston's Logan International Airport and to spend all the time it took to bang out an agreement. We both wanted to start at the top! Many issues were involved, not the least of which were the production schedule and the pricing. Mirro and I felt that it wouldn't serve any purpose to meet at lower levels. This meeting was a fantastic success. We hashed out our respective problems and agreed to a price. It turns out that Armourcote II was our most successful product ever. Armourcote II sales totaled $80 million dollars. Isn't it amazing what a raw chicken can do? Isn't it also amazing what starting at the top can do?

Start at the Top

Remember, no matter what problem you are having or situation you are dealing with, if you want the best and fastest results in the least amount of time, "start at the top!"

Armourcote II cookware.

Armourcote bakeware.

The Wisdom of Ginsu

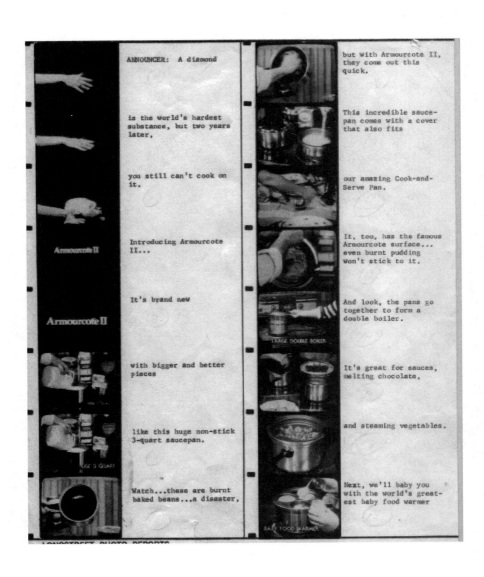

ANNOUNCER: A diamond

is the world's hardest substance, but two years later,

you still can't cook on it.

Introducing Armourcote II...

It's brand new

with bigger and better pieces

like this huge non-stick 3-quart saucepan.

Watch...these are burnt baked beans...a disaster,

but with Armourcote II, they come out this quick.

This incredible sauce-pan comes with a cover that also fits

our amazing Cook-and-Serve Pan.

It, too, has the famous Armourcote surface... even burnt pudding won't stick to it.

And look, the pans go together to form a double boiler.

It's great for sauces, melting chocolate,

and steaming vegetables.

Next, we'll baby you with the world's great-est baby food warmer

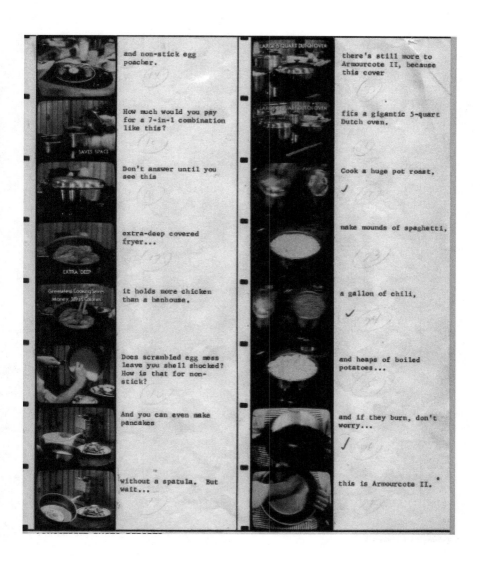

and non-stick egg poacher.

How much would you pay for a 7-in-1 combination like this?

Don't answer until you see this

extra-deep covered fryer...

it holds more chicken than a henhouse.

Does scrambled egg mess leave you shell shocked? How is that for non-stick?

And you can even make pancakes

without a spatula. But wait...

there's still more to Armourcote II, because this cover

fits a gigantic 5-quart Dutch oven.

Cook a huge pot roast,

make mounds of spaghetti,

a gallon of chili,

and heaps of boiled potatoes...

and if they burn, don't worry...

this is Armourcote II.

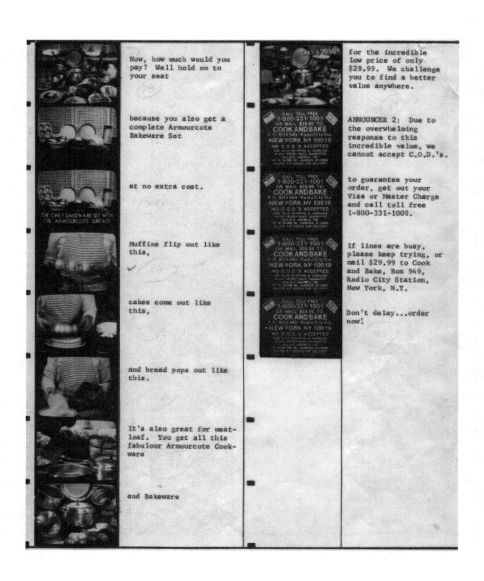

Now, how much would you pay? Well hold on to your seat

because you also get a complete Armourcote Bakeware Set

at no extra cost.

Muffins flip out like this,

cakes come out like this,

and bread pops out like this.

It's also great for meat-loaf. You get all this fabulour Armourcote Cookware

and Bakeware

for the incredible low price of only $29.99. We challenge you to find a better value anywhere.

ANNOUNCER 2: Due to the overwhelming response to this incredible value, we cannot accept C.O.D.'s.

to guarantee your order, get out your Visa or Master Charge and call toll free 1-800-331-1001.

If lines are busy, please keep trying, or mail $29.99 to Cook and Bake, Box 949, Radio City Station, New York, N.Y.

Don't delay...order now!

Know What Buttons to Push...and Push Them

Barry

Everyone should learn as much as possible about what motivates the people with whom they are dealing. This information should be used to your advantage. Parents start teaching their children how to push their teachers' buttons at an early age. That's where the idea of bringing the teacher an apple came from. Some wise parent saw the opportunity to separate her child from the rest of the children in the teacher's mind. All she had to do was have little Johnnie bring his teacher an apple.

This process works in the business world also. If your boss is a football fan, it is imperative that you find out what team he roots for and become a fan of that team also. Learn the names of the players, their statistics, and the standings. Even if you hate football, watch his favorite team play. On Monday cry with him over the loss, or smile with him over the win. Discuss the great plays. Push the right button and your future will get brighter.

If your boss is female, find out what turns her on. If it's not football, maybe it's clothing, jewelry, wine, or children. Whatever it is, learn all you can about it. Mention it and discuss it. Questions and comments such as, "Is that a new handbag?" or "My child had open house at school this week, did yours?" or "What a beautiful bracelet that is. Does it have any special meaning?" can go a long way toward establishing a good relationship. These are surefire buttons to push and will ingratiate you with the recipient.

Most people (especially those who would never think of doing it) call this "sucking up" or "brownnosing," but what it really should be called is "intelligent thinking." Have you ever met a boss—or a spouse—who didn't think he or she deserved to be treated special or got upset with you for knowing what he or she liked? In fact, as illustrated by a study published in the August 2004 issue of the *Journal of Applied Psychology*, knowing how to "push the right buttons" can not only help you keep a job and get ahead in it, it can also help you get the right job in the first place! Researchers go on to say that brownnosing was more likely to leave a favorable impression with interviewers than self-promotion in job interviews.

Of course, buttons can be used in reverse to tick people off. Some people call it sarcasm, but reverse button-pushing is much more than that. A really effective reverse button-pusher is George Steinbrenner. He's known to be the toughest baseball team owner in the world. At one time his manager would take the Yankees within an eyelash of winning the World Series and lose in the seventh game of the series. What would Steinbrenner do? Instead of congratulating his manager for having a great year and almost winning the World Series, he would fire him. That's the ultimate in reverse button-pushing. A demotion of job title has the same effect.

There are much more subtle ways to push a negative button and motivate people. Let's face it, parents have been using negative button-pushing forever.

"Finish your homework or no TV tonight!"

"Take out the garbage before you play any video games!"

"You can have that new sweater you want if you get an A on your math test!"

If your boss comes in and starts yelling because something has gone wrong, he's pushing everybody's buttons!

Ed

Pick up any book on the art of the negotiation and it will tell you that a good deal is when both sides win. Some people tend to negotiate by telling you up front what they want; others choose to reveal their needs slowly, sizing up their opponents to gauge their weaknesses. Here's a tactic that we had the misfortune to experience first-hand. It was so shocking to me at the time that I still consider it to be one of the most memorable negotiating tactics I have ever experienced: I call it "pulling a Ray Kives." Here's how it happened. One of our partners, Phil Felstead, had been approached by K-Tel International in England. K-Tel, as you may remember was one of the first companies in the United States to introduce and sell record compilations. Most of us grew up watching these record compilation offers on TV. They offered classics such as the greatest hits of the '60s and '70s and the greatest hits of one particular star, such as Neil Diamond. K-Tel advertised their offers on TV, but unlike us, sold their records in retail, mostly in drugstore and specialty chain stores across the country. They had a substantial lock on the marketplace with massive distribution, good rack-space exposure, and a constant flurry of commercials on TV. In fact, as a sales representative for the NBC affiliate in Providence I made quite a bit of commission placing K-Tel advertisements on my station. We learned from Philip that K-Tel had explained to him in a London meeting the need to break into other types of merchandise besides records and that the Miracle Painter was on their radar screen. Because we had already been very successful in TV mail-order, getting the product in retail seemed to be a natural extension. Obviously, when K-Tel expressed interest in sitting down to talk to us we were excited. They invited us to visit their world headquarters in Winnipeg, Canada. When the four of us arrived that day in Canada we had no idea what was in store for us. If we had, we would have gotten back on the plane and flew home.

I met Barry, Mickey, and Phil at the Providence Airport at 6 a.m. for an early morning flight to Chicago. From there it was another flight to Winnipeg. We jumped in a cab for the ride to K-Tel headquarters and upon arrival all of us were extremely impressed with the sprawling headquarters of K-Tel International. We were led through a monstrous warehouse to the executive office section of the building. Then we were ushered into the largest private offices we had ever seen. Phillip Kives's (the president of K-Tel) office seemed to be as large as a house. Behind his gigantic desk sat Phillip. We introduced ourselves and he told us to have a seat. We looked around for chairs, but there weren't any. Phillip looked at us amusingly and pointed to a couch and chairs about 30 feet away from his desk. We took the long walk to the couch and plopped onto it. Phillip excused himself and disappeared for about half an hour. When he came back we discussed our proposal. We would let him use our commercial and we would also sell him the Miracle Painters. K-Tel would advertise the product on TV in the United Kingdom and also make sure that the shelves of its retail stores were stocked with the product. That was our proposal. Enter Ray Kives. Phillip Kives said that we should run the deal by his brother Ray because Ray was the financial guy. He paged Ray, and a few minutes later he showed up. We went through the details of the deal once again. Ray wanted to know about the pricing. He asked us, "How much are you making on each Miracle Painter?"

Barry replied, "50 cents."

Ray's face turned red and he said, "Are you kidding? You shouldn't be making more than a dime! I could have them made in Korea for a lot less."

What happened next was astonishing to all of us. Ray said, "Would you excuse me for a minute?" and left the room.

We thought he might be discussing the issue with his brother or someone else. After about 30 minutes, we became concerned. After 45 minutes, one of us opened the door to his office and said to his secretary, "Is Mr. Kives coming back soon?"

Know What Buttons to Push...and Push Them

She replied "Oh no! Mr. Kives left 45 minutes ago. He went home." We asked her to call us a taxi and left for the airport. Apparently he didn't like the price we offered.

Talk about pushing buttons! He sure pushed ours! Here we had traveled halfway across the country, took two planes, got up at 4 in the morning, and this guy just goes home. Unbelievable! But he sure knew what he was doing. He was holding all the cards and he played them his way. He knew that we needed him more than he needed us. He had made up his mind that 10 cents was what he wanted to pay and we didn't have enough leverage over him to negotiate. He had done his homework on us. Leaving the room was such a profound way of expressing that point, but the point, nonetheless, was made in a big way.

Of course, you don't *have* to leave a room the way Ray Kives did to make a point or gain the advantage in a negotiation. In fact, it's a rather extreme method of negotiating, but the logic behind the maneuver is sound. Know where you stand with the person who or parties that you are about to negotiate with. Ask yourself, "Do I have strength in this meeting or does my opponent?" Try to mentally put yourself in the mindset of your opponent. How would you respond to your requests? How will you respond to his requests? Role-play the possibilities in your mind and, most importantly, eliminate the emotions that constantly get in the way of good negotiations. That way the buttons that you are looking for will reveal themselves so that you can push them.

I always try to negotiate from a position of strength. When I am not in that enviable position, I never reveal it. I am also prepared to walk away from a deal, like Ray Kives did, to make a point.

Remember, half the battle in winning any negotiation is "knowing what buttons to push...and pushing them!"

Keep the "Chainge"

Barry

We had been selling on television primarily things that can be used in the kitchen. Whenever we parted from that room we lost money. We lost money on the Dog Talk album, an album that was recorded by a dog psychologist and taught you how to understand what your dog was saying to you. We also lost money on Elvis Presley and Star Wars jewelry. Another loser was the golf swing monitor. It was supposed to help improve your golf swing. The only thing that improved was our ability to lose money. But one day Ron Verri, the brother of our attorney, Bob Verri, came to us with a unique gold-plated necklace. What was unique about it, you ask?

The Wisdom of Ginsu

Through slides on the chain, the necklace could be changed into many different sizes and shapes. It could be a regular necklace. It could be a double loop necklace. It could even change into a bracelet. Ed was extremely impressed with it; I was somewhat reluctant. We were presented with the product at a time when Ed and his family and my family were going on school vacation to our condos in Florida. We had vacation condos in the same Ft. Lauderdale development. While we were there, Ed did his own form of focus group work. He would walk up to each and every woman sitting at the pool and have her try on the necklace. He would find out if they liked the concept of an adjustable necklace and also how much they would be willing to pay for it. He would then ask them if they would buy it for $19.95, $29.95, and even $39.95. When we went into restaurants he would pull the same routine. After a week of this type of questioning he said, "I think we might have a profitable product here." Ever the cautionary one, I reminded him of our past failures whenever we made a move out of the kitchen. He still felt strongly that we should give it a try. As always, when one of us had a good feeling about a product we went forward with it. We weren't afraid to change. We needed a name for the product, so we called it Chainge, a play on the words chain and change. We came up with the line, "Isn't it time you had a Chainge?" We hired a beautiful model who was also a New England Patriots cheerleader to appear in the commercial and had her pose with the necklace on while the announcer said, "We'll go to any length to please you." The video showed a hand pulling on the Chainge and forcing it from a double necklace to a long, single necklace. The price we decided on was $19.95. It sold like hotcakes. Before we knew it, it was taking in more than a million dollars a month.

We decided to change again when an enterprising young fellow from South Africa came to see us with an interesting calculator watch. We loved this guy. He looked as if he had just come out of the Australian bush: long blonde hair, semi-military type of garb, and a demeanor and smile similar to Australian actor Paul Hogan.

At that time, the only calculator watch on the market was made by Casio and cost $50. He told us that he could sell us a calculator watch with more features than Casio's watch for about $7. Being a tech junkie, I fell in love with the watch. It also occurred to me that if we bought it for $7, we could probably sell it for $20 or $30 and undercut Casio's price. We might have another winner if we changed once again from our normal product line.

We figured "what the heck," let's make a commercial. After all, *Chainge* was good! The creative department wanted to make a commercial that showed all the features of the watch and they wanted to show its 20 features with all shots being filmed on location. For example, we would show the stopwatch with runners running a race, military time with soldiers saluting a flag, and so forth. We had just made a commercial for the Sky-Fi Solar Radio Visor and had shot the whole commercial on location, which had cost about four times what our other in-studio commercials had cost.

Ever the anchor who didn't want to spend a lot of money on production, I refused to budge from my position that we could fasten the watch to a piece of colored cardboard and show all its 20 features by doing a voiceover and special effects with the watch tied down in one place. I won this battle and we ended up making a great (inexpensive) commercial without leaving the studio. We called it the Multichron watch and marketed it as having 20 features ranging from a stopwatch to dual alarms to 12- or 24-hour military time being displayed. We even had a bonus 21st feature. It was the price: only $24.99.

This change was really good for us, as the product took in about $10 million before everyone and their brother started importing similar watches from Hong Kong and flooded the retail market with them.

Think of what would have happened if we weren't willing to change our product selection.

Ed

There is an old saying: "The only thing constant is change." Then there is my favorite saying, the definition of insanity. What is it? "Keep doing the same thing over and over again and expect different results." I constantly see this in the ad business. I see many businesses (not my clients) advertise using the same old copy, using the same medium, and spending the same budget, and then saying, "My business is not what it used to be. What's happening?" What is happening is that your competition is doing something different. They are changing. Perhaps they are conforming to a changing market place, a changing customer base, a different economy, or have created a new concept that has caught on! They are doing all of this and at the same time cleaning your clock.

So, don't be afraid to change. Rediscover yourself. Reinvent yourself. We've done it throughout our careers and discovered this pearl of wisdom in the process: Whether it's your business, your approach, your personal life, or your staff, you've got to mix things up a little every now and then and change.

Change is good, so "keep the 'Chainge.'"

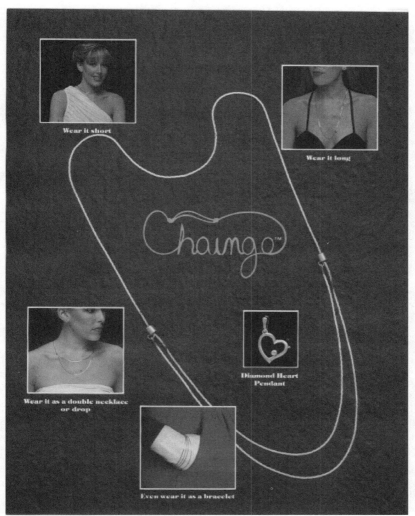

The Chainge.

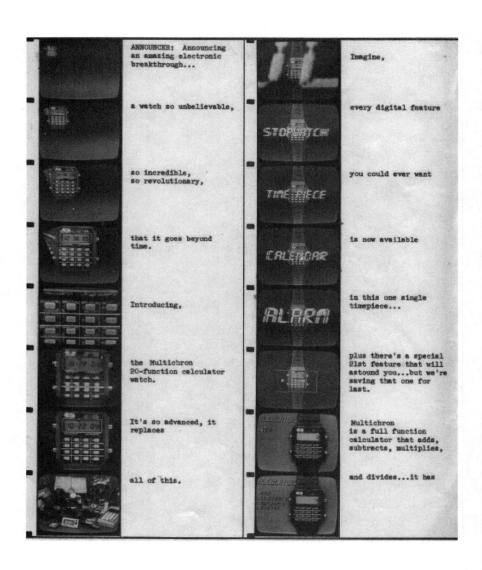

ANNOUNCER: Announcing an amazing electronic breakthrough...

a watch so unbelievable,

so incredible, so revolutionary,

that it goes beyond time.

Introducing,

the Multichron 20-function calculator watch.

It's so advanced, it replaces

all of this.

Imagine,

every digital feature

you could ever want

is now available

in this one single timepiece...

plus there's a special 21st feature that will astound you...but we're saving that one for last.

Multichron is a full function calculator that adds, subtracts, multiplies,

and divides...it has

STOPWATCH

TIME PIECE

CALENDAR

ALARM

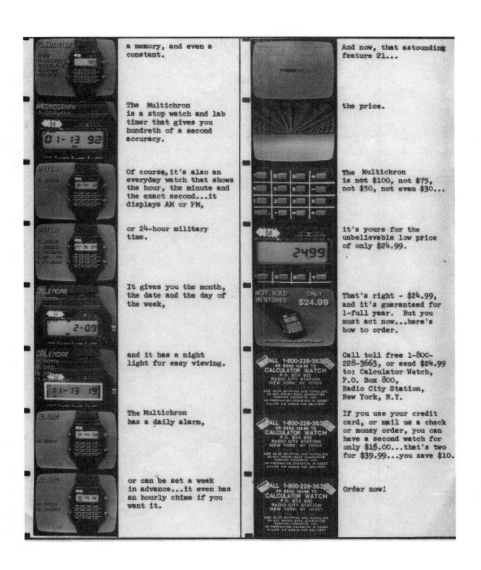

a memory, and even a constant.

The Multichron is a stop watch and lab timer that gives you hundredth of a second accuracy.

Of course, it's also an everyday watch that shows the hour, the minute and the exact second...it displays AM or PM,

or 24-hour military time.

It gives you the month, the date and the day of the week,

and it has a night light for easy viewing.

The Multichron has a daily alarm,

or can be set a week in advance...it even has an hourly chime if you want it.

And now, that astounding feature 21...

the price.

The Multichron is not $100, not $75, not $50, not even $30...

it's yours for the unbelievable low price of only $24.99.

That's right - $24.99, and it's guaranteed for 1-full year. But you must act now...here's how to order.

Call toll free 1-800-228-3663, or send $24.99 to: Calculator Watch, P.O. Box 800, Radio City Station, New York, N.Y.

If you use your credit card, or mail us a check or money order, you can have a second watch for only $15.00...that's two for $39.99...you save $10.

Order now!

Know a Little About as Many Things as Possible

Barry

The more you know, the more chances you're going to know something about a subject that interests a person you may be working with or doing business with. In every field, being able to converse with many people on a variety of subjects endears you to those in attendance, because people love talking about things that they're interested in. Don't you?

If 10 people want to do business with someone and they all have equal skills and abilities, what's the tie-breaker going to be?

Let's face it, being on the same wavelength with your boss, your friends, and your associates can be a valuable thing. Having common interests with a person elevates you in his eyes and makes you more approachable and likable. Over the years we've had teachers who we liked and teachers who liked us. Somehow, it always seemed to be easier to get a higher grade in classes where the teachers liked us. It is the same way in the business world. If your supervisors like you, it is easier to get ahead. If they really like you, it is even easier. If they don't, well, you already know the answer to that. So the question becomes, how do you get your coworkers, supervisors, clients, and even friends to like you? One sure way is to show an interest in things they like and to know a little about a lot of things sure helps. It gives you the opportunity to enter a conversation on almost any subject and be a participant.

Ed

My daughter, who just graduated from Harvard University, had such a diverse choice of freshman elective seminars that anyone examining these choices from the outside would have to wonder how any student was going to even begin to decide which one of the 116 classes available (ranging from Bob Dylan and Chess and Mathematics to Slovakian Languages and Water on Mars) to choose. Even more mystifying to me was how she was going to learn about any particular subject in-depth when there were so many different areas to consider. However, in attending a freshman/parent dinner one evening, the dean of the college said, "We want your children to learn a little about a lot of things now, and when they graduate, learn a lot about a little in graduate school. In other words, Harvard undergrads experience the range of courses the same way one would sample an appetizer table. Then select the main course later."

In my opinion, that's exactly how anyone who wants to get ahead in business—and in life—should approach the thousands of news, sports, lifestyles, hobby, business, financial, entertainment, and various other subjects that the media and people around you talk about every single day. Whether you get your daily informational fix from the newspaper, radio, television, other people, or the Internet, knowing a little about a lot will carry you a very long way.

Barry

Ed is a master in the study of knowing a little about as many things as possible. He sucks up information like an anteater in the middle of an ant farm, and he remembers most everything he reads. Do you know enough to hold your own in a cocktail party setting? Could you jump in on any conversation and feel comfortable? To make a good impression, you need to be able to have this skill and knowledge. Ed's favorite technique is scanning the newspaper headlines on a daily basis and watching headline news. In less than half an hour a day Ed is prepared to enter any conversation.

He has practically no interest in sports but he can tell you who is in first place in any sport and can tell you the position of the local team. Because of his ability to know a little about many things, he is able to connect with almost anyone and have an intelligent conversation on virtually any subject.

Ed's technique works for me also. I may not know all the details, but at least I don't have the "deer in the headlights" glaze when some subject is mentioned. Plus someone is always willing to talk if you give them the opening: just say, "What are your views on this?" By listening intently to the answer, Ed gains even more information that can be used to extend the conversation.

In no time at all you'll be up to speed on the entire conversation. If you find you still don't know enough about what's being discussed, you can always say, "That's interesting. I don't know as much about that subject as you do, so I am pleased to be your student and be educated." That at least gives you the appearance of being sophisticated, intelligent, and interested in the subject matter, while passing off a well-deserved compliment.

This especially helps when talking to future clients, people you are trying to sell or impress, or even a future boss.

Ed

Barry's no slouch when it comes to knowing a little about a lot. In fact, there are quite a few things he knows a lot about as well!

His wife, Leslie, has often told me how amazed she is when he enters into conversations at weddings and other social events where she is sure he knows nothing about the subject. She has mentioned many times that she was startled when he participated with substantial knowledge in subjects as varied as medicine, astronomy, scuba diving, and aeronautics.

Then there is the case of Barry's friend Gary Lorden. Gary is a professor of mathematics at Caltech. Let's face it, the first image that pops into your mind when you think of a professor of mathematics is a nerd with a plastic pocket protector loaded with pens and pencils. In many cases, you would be right. In Gary's case, you would be very, very wrong. Gary is one of those rare people who knows a lot about a lot of things and a little about everything else. He is a phenomenal piano player and an excellent singer. He has appeared in many acting performances and can deliver a joke like the best comedians. He can easily discuss football, baseball, basketball, and hockey as well as politics, history, science, and medicine. It seems like there is no gathering or discussion that Gary can't participate in. It is certainly no wonder that at Caltech Gary has been the head of the math department, dean of students, and vice president for student affairs.

Barry

This Ginsuism of "knowing a little about as many things as possible" helped to achieve remarkable results by having many of the people we did business with enjoy the experience. Before any meeting, we would try to learn as much about the company as we could and the people running it. They would always be blown away by our knowledge of their business and, in some cases, of their personal career achievements.

I am always impressed when I interview someone and I ask, "Do you have any questions about the company?"

And the person says something along these lines: "I am well acquainted with your company. In fact, I spent a great deal of time on your Website. I was most impressed to read your views on direct marketing in the last issue of *DM* magazine. I share your views on that subject." That person then goes on to mention our other achievements, awards, and success and engage me in the conversation by allowing me to talk more about myself. Now all of this information about us is on our Website and archived in libraries, but this person took the time to learn it, remember it, and use it to impress. That's certainly much more desirable than having someone say, "No, I don't know anything about you or the company. Why don't you tell me?"

So, remember, "know a little about as many things as possible!"

Bonus Ginsuism

Ed

Now, did you pick up a bit of Ginsu wisdom from all of the examples in this book? Good, because learning all that wisdom cost us about 30 years and millions of dollars. Now, how much would you pay for some additional wisdom? Okay, okay, you already bought the book. *But wait! There's more!* You've been such an attentive reader that Barry and I are going to throw in this special, bonus Ginsuism, a $40 value, absolutely free! But you must read on, *now!*

How to get people to return your phone calls.

Now that you know the importance of returning your calls, here's a surefire way to have the people who don't return calls return yours. How? Send them the GOYF. It's not Yiddish, it's "Ginsuish" for "get off your fax."

The Wisdom of Ginsu

I credit this clever idea to one of my best friends, Harvey Adelberg. He used it successfully on a number of tough customers over the years. As you can see, it's timeless, and so is he.

(Company Name)Fax

To: Person who doesn't call back

From: Tired of waiting

Subject: Soon to be fired

Message: Dear Person Who Doesn't Call Back, (insert real name)

Subject: My Proposal

As you know, I have tried numerous times to reach you on the phone. So in an effort to get an answer on the proposal I sent you, could you please just check one of the boxes below and fax back to me? Thanks in advance.

P.S. My boss said my job is on the line if I don't get an answer because he/she thinks I'm out playing golf instead of trying to reach you.

Check one of the choices below:

(_____) Dear Tired of Waiting: I have been so swamped with work that I haven't even called my (___)wife, (___) mistress, (_____) girlfriend, (___) boyfriend, (_____)all of the above back. So what does that tell you? I am interested, so keep trying.

(_____) Dear Tired of Waiting: I am not busy. I am not returning your calls because I don't like you! In fact, I don't like your company, your wife, your kids, or your dog. By the way, as far as I'm concerned, you can gas up the dinghy and go fishing with Fredo, because you are dead to me! Do not try contacting me again.

The copy above is just one suggestion. This almost always gets a response—good or bad! But we encourage you to be creative and do what works best and feels most natural for you! Most people just find this too funny to ignore, and a few just don't like it all. However, we're going with the percentages, as it has opened many a closed door for us.

Remember, if people aren't getting back to you, they may be busy; they may not be interested; or they may even be ill, away, or dealing with matters far more important than what you have to say. But if you're persistent, get their attention, stand out from the crowd, and make them laugh, no matter how you do it, you have a very good chance to get an answer. So what have you got to lose?

Remember this Bonus Ginsuism when you are having a tough time getting a call or e-mail back from someone.

Thank you for reading this book,
and good luck living the Ginsu way of life!

If you would like to order a copy of the g roundbreaking commercials mentioned in this book, please call 1-800-397-5804.

Index

About the Authors

Barry Becher is the cocreator of some of the most recognizable direct response products and commercials in television history. The Ginsu knife, Armourcote cookware, The Miracle Painter, The Miracle Slicer, Lustreware silverware, and Royal DuraSteel mixing bowls are just a few of the creations he helped mastermind.

He is an accomplished copywriter, media buyer/planner, and results analyst. He has served as president and CFO of the various corporations that he has developed over the years. Barry's nationally renowned marketing talents, achievements, and expertise in media buying have been recognized via seven ECHO Awards for order generation, as well as numerous New England Direct Marketing Association (NEDMA), Hatch, U.S. Television, and Advertising Age awards.

He and his work have appeared in numerous documentaries on ABC-TV, The History Channel, The Discovery Channel, and A&E.

An avid computer enthusiast since the advent of the microcomputer (1976), Barry has developed software used to verify credit cards and locate media invoice discrepancies.

Barry has also served as a media strategy consultant to the Democratic National Committee and as a judge for the International ECHO Awards.

Prior to teaming with Ed Valenti, he was the owner of several national franchise operations. He has served as president of the Rhode Island Pilots Association and, with more than 2,000 hours as pilot in command, has flown everything from single-engine aircraft to jets. Barry holds an airplane speed record from Oklahoma City, Oklahoma, to Memphis, Tennessee. He is also an accomplished scuba diver and has had the opportunity to dive at exotic locales around the globe.

About the Authors

Ed Valenti began his broadcast career as a disc jockey and rapidly rose through the ranks to attain key executive sales positions with Capitol Cities/ABC/Disney and NBC Television.

He is widely recognized as a direct marketing industry pioneer, having introduced concepts such as credit card order-taking and the use of toll-free numbers on television.

Ed is also responsible for creating some of America's most well-known and profitable advertising campaigns, including the legendary Ginsu knife, which went on to become one of the most successful products in television advertising history. In addition, he has worked as a direct marketing consultant to the Independent Television Companies in London, England.

He is currently COO and cofounder of PriMedia Inc., a national media buying and marketing firm working on some of America's best-known companies and brand names, and a keynote speaker on the lecture circuit.

Ed is the past recipient of numerous industry awards, including 11 International ECHO Awards, as well as numerous awards from the New England Direct Marketing Association, U.S. Television Commercials Festival, Advertising Age, and the Hatch Awards for creative excellence. He has also served as a judge for the National Emmy and International ECHO Awards.

Ed has also appeared in numerous documentaries on national television networks ranging from ABC (Chronicle) and The History Channel to The Discovery Channel and the A&E network. His work has also been featured on VH1's *Pop-Up Videos* and *I love the 80's*, *The Sopranos*, *Saturday Night Live*, *The Tonight Show*, and numerous motion pictures.

He has been happily married for more than 30 years and has two beautiful daughters.